WRITING TO TEACH; WRITING TO LEARN IN HIGHER EDUCATION

Susan M. Leist

University Press of America,® Inc.
Lanham · Boulder · New York · Toronto · Oxford

Copyright © 2006 by
University Press of America,® Inc.
4501 Forbes Boulevard
Suite 200
Lanham, Maryland 20706
UPA Acquisitions Department (301) 459-3366

PO Box 317
Oxford
OX2 9RU, UK

Library of Congress Control Number: 2005906167
ISBN 0-7618-3322-6 (clothbound : alk. ppr.)
ISBN 0-7618-3323-4 (paperback : alk. ppr.)

47.00

TABLE OF CONTENTS

PREFACE

Dear Colleague:

The use of writing to teach and learn has become common practice in education because writing is among the most effective teaching and learning tools in existence. If you are interested in using writing to teach, you will find the contents of this teaching guide useful. The book contains a full range materials dealing with meeting the everyday needs of a writing-emphasis course. When one comes to understand the endless applications of the techniques, one can revitalize any classroom and influence student reading, writing, and critical thinking profoundly.

One section of this book contains sample "W" Course Guidelines.

These standards are intended to be interpreted by teachers according to their discipline and the nature of their assignments. The primary consideration, then, in determining acceptability for student writing should be whether or not the writing communicates clearly and effectively within the context of the discipline.

A significant feature of all guidelines for "W" courses is the requirement that required formal writing display some evidence of critical thinking. Thought-provoking, creative assignments based on the course objectives are likely to stimulate that kind of response from students more than conventional assignments such as term papers and book reviews. Additionally, teachers are encouraged to incorporate within their course plans a variety of informal, ungraded writing activities to stimulate student involvement and better learning.

Teachers of writing intensive courses, therefore, are encouraged to refuse acceptance of papers which are poorly written and to require students to seek help before revising and resubmitting their work. This book includes a number of suggestions for planning interesting assignments, using writing in the classroom, and responding to student writing, both graded and ungraded. I hope you will find the book useful. Good luck!

-Susan M. Leist
Buffalo, New York

ACKNOWLEDGEMENTS

Conceptually, this guidebook owes much to a publication titled *Writing/Learning: Using Writing in the Classroom,* a faculty handbook written by Patricia D'Urfee and Anne Sowa and printed only on the campus for the use of the faculty at Broome Community College. I saw it during their presentation at a State University of New York Council on Writing conference in 1993.

The present text was produced in cooperation with SUNY College at Buffalo faculty members who participated in intensive workshops concerning the use of writing to teach held between 1991 and 1999. Many of their course plans employing techniques for using writing to teach are contained in this book as examples. These professors agreed to serve as practicing consultants for other SUCB faculty interested in learning and using the techniques of writing to teach, for they see writing as a highly efficient pedagogical tool. They believe that the use of writing as a teaching tool is vitally important to any institution. Having learned much about using writing to teach during the workshops, they have continued learning as they implement their knowledge in their own classrooms. I appreciated their enthusiastic participation and their help. I also appreciated the contribution of sample checklists given to me by Dr. Thomas Reigstad and the feedback given to me by Dr. Barbara Bontempo, both of the S.U.C.B. English Department.

An earlier version of this work was published in 1997 by Simon and Schuster Custom Publishing under the title, A Guidebook for Using Writing to Teach Across the Curriculum. The present version is newly organized, contains new examples, materials and bibliography. The rhetorical materials used here can be found in many other places, but they have been re-conceptualized and re-organized for application to disciplinary writing as a learning tool.

CHAPTER I

THE WRITING PROCESS

In the past thirty years or so, the theory concerning how people write has undergone enormous change. There are hundreds of studies and books exploring this theory. Some are listed in the bibliography for this book. If you are interested in enlarging your awareness, it would be worth your time to read some of them. They all work from an essential premise–that writing is a recursive process. When a piece of writing is taken through the complete process, the end product is error-free writing which has been thought about and revised so that its potential has been explored.

The Writing Process consists of several stages:

Pre-writing: Using some writing technique or exercise to begin the process by exploring ideas, establishing an approach, finding or inventing material, or assimilating ideas and material into an individual's own learning system. (Pre-writing techniques may also be employed for myriad other purposes.)

Drafting: The first "write-through", drawing on, organizing and extending pre-writing materials. (Sometimes this turns out to be the only "write-through" as in an essay examination.)

Revising: Returning to a first draft and altering it in various ways. Revision always involves considering the needs of a potential reader; those needs will govern much of what is added to or cut from a first draft! Revision also may involve addressing the responses of a peer reader or a teacher to a draft. It may mean elaboration, incorporating new material–from other sources or the writer's own discovery. It may involve "tightening", cutting out extraneous words or redundancies. It may involve exploring the pieces that don't fit just to see how they might change the writing. Although errors may get corrected in the course of the revision stage, error correction is not the primary consideration of revision!

Editing: This is the stage for error correction. The last thing the writer does prior to submitting a piece of writing, whether to a teacher for a grade or to an editor for publication, is to get the writing error-free and in the required format. Editing is the responsibility of writers. If they cannot do their own editing efficiently, then they need to seek help in getting it done. Teachers should only edit their students' work by their own choice.

These stages of the writing process are sometimes expressed in different terminology. Pre-writing, for example, is sometimes called "invention" or "rehearsing". They are always, though, some version of the above stages. It is important to remember, when one thinks about writing, that these stages are recursive. Writers do not proceed in orderly fashion through the process. They may use only part of the process. For example, when students answer an essay question on a timed exam, they are only using the drafting stage of writing. The question itself is the pre-writing stage; there is not much time for revision or editing.

Also, writers may draft and then decide to change their minds about something they have said in the draft during the revision stage. This may cause re-drafting in an entirely new direction. In fact, it may elicit new pre-writing to get started in that new direction. So it goes, back and forth on a zig-zag path as far as writers need to go in the process. In the use of writing to teach, much informal writing would be classed as pre-writing, for it is writing to discover or to put things together in some order.

When professors do scholarly writing, they usually go back and forth in the process many times. They get an idea or perceive patterns in some set of variables. That is a process in itself which usually takes some time. They read what others may have said germane to their topic, and they assimilate their reading into their thinking. They may do some other kind of research in the process to incorporate in the piece. Then they write a draft which they may bring to a colleague for responses. They go back to the piece, considering the responses, and re-work it. They may do this several times before they have a revised piece to submit to a journal or publisher. That revised piece may be quite different from the initial draft, for writers learn more about the subject of their writing as they go. To get the piece ready for submission, they assure themselves that it is as error-free as possible and that it is in the format of a particular publisher's manuscript guidelines.

This process of scholarly writing is, after all, what you want your students to carry out also, in the context of your courses. You are better at it than your students for you are functioning at a higher level, but basically the process is the same for your students as for you.

When you begin to think about your writing processes as being the same as your students', then the use of writing to teach and to learn becomes a clearer topic. Besides your fully processed scholarly writing, you do a great amount of writing which you do not take through the whole process; you want them to do that, too. You make notes about things. You write memos. You write syllabi with objectives and procedures. You write lists. If you think, you can come up with a dozen ways that you use writing in your professional life, writing that is never fully processed. You might look at it as writing that is not done for a "grade", but rather for other purposes. Writing is your major operating tool.

Rather than being "taught to write" through this kind of writing, you are writing to teach yourself, to learn. This, too, should be the same for students, should it not?

The purpose of this guidebook is to make you aware not only of writing as a process, but of writing as a teaching/learning tool. You can inject writing to teach into your pedagogy in a multitude of ways. If you are limiting the writing in your courses to the "term paper" and some essay questions on tests, then you are depriving your students as well as yourself. You can foster your students' development as scholars by showing them writing as a powerful learning tool. Your primary operating tool can become theirs, also.

For many faculty across the disciplines, the prospect of using writing to teach is intimidating for they think that demanding writing from students means faculty become involved mainly in correcting student errors; error correction takes an inordinate amount of time. Teachers sometimes feel inadequate to the task.

One of this book's messages is good news for those people. Although error-free text is a desirable end product, *error correction is the "janitorial" work of composition.* The instructor has a choice as to whether or not to correct student work. A more productive use of instructional time would be to set up situations where students have audiences other than the teacher for their fully processed writing. The teacher could help get student texts ready for an outside audience, advising students that errors exist in them and informing as to where they might find copy-editing help to correct those errors. Teachers who choose may do copy-editing for their students; they are not obligated to. Copy-editing by a teacher should be looked upon as an indication that a teacher cares enough to help students rather than as the instructor's responsibility. Using writing to teach is much different from error correction.

CREATING THE WRITING INTENSIVE COURSE

Too often on campuses where writing-across-the-curriculum programs are not well articulated, professors will elect to teach writing intensive courses because enrollment numbers are limited in them–not because the professors are interested in using writing to teach. These courses are taught then as regular courses with the add-on of a paper as a course component. Usually, this situation produces an experience for both student and teacher which has little resemblance to a writing intensive course.

Writing intensive courses should be courses in which the components include the use of writing to teach and learn. Professors teaching them should be, above all, committed to the fostering of student voice and should be able to view their students as people like themselves. The fostering of independent scholarship among students should be among their top priorities. In the service of that priority, they should seek ways by which they can share the responsibility with students–both for learning and for evaluation.

These professors need to have command of techniques of heuristic writing. They should understand the differences between informal writing and formal writing. They should understand the writing process and its advantages to them and to students. They should intentionally inject heuristic writing into their pedagogy whenever it can be profitably used. They should be cognizant of the importance of assignment creation and should be willing to spend the extra planning time involved in writing effective assignments. They should understand the connections between assignment and evaluation.

Since you are reading this book, you either are a professor who has this combination of knowledge and attitudes or you want to be such a professor. Perhaps you teach on a campus which has a well-established and defined WAC program. If so, then this book will assist you in becoming part of that program, and you may want to compare your campus guidelines for its writing intensive program to the sample guidelines which follow. If not, then you perhaps you can be instrumental in creating a WAC or writing intensive program on your campus. In this case, the sample guidelines may be useful to you as a model. These guidelines also contain suggestions for departmental options for portfolios of student writing used as a graduation requirement. Such portfolios would be products of a WAC program:

SAMPLE GUIDELINES FOR "W" COURSES, WRITING INTENSIVE COURSES AND DEPARTMENTAL OPTIONS

A college might require that students meet a writing intensive requirement by one of two methods: (1) taking writing intensive courses, or (2) fulfilling a departmental option such as a graduation portfolio. Most campuses now have some version of these requirements.

The first method requires taking two "W" courses as a part of the undergraduate studies at the college. Writing intensive course sections are marked W in the college's schedule of courses. "W" courses are offered by each department so that students will have adequate opportunities to take such courses as they pursue the requirements for an undergraduate degree in their chosen fields. It is possible that students could take both "W" courses within their programs or both outside their programs and still meet the requirements.

Like most courses offered on campus, "W" courses include both formal and informal writing. Writing intensive courses, however, emphasize writing as a major course component for both instruction and evaluation. Writing intensive courses are those in which professors employ writing-to-learn techniques as a major means of delivering instruction. Such courses include teaching students to use writing as a tool in their overall learning process. Students can bolster their general academic abilities greatly by taking these courses.

Sample "W" Course Rationale and Components

1. Amount and type of writing.

a. A writing intensive course includes several assignments using formal writing; formal writing, in this context, means writing which is intended to communicate with a reader, which has been revised, and which meets standards for minimum proficiency. The formal writing requirement should be substantial enough to insure that the "W" courses function effectively as part of a writing program which begins in Freshman Composition. Formal writing requires students to write for a specific audience, and thus prepares them for effective communication in the academic and professional worlds they will encounter after college. Minimum standards of proficiency are important to help students understand what is normally expected from a college graduate and assure the faculty that graduates are literate.

b. Many types of writing assignments can meet the "W" requirements for formal writing including: term papers, lab report discussions, short essays, book reviews, article summaries, reports, micro-themes, annotated bibliographies, etc. "W" courses are not term paper centered. Rather, "W" course instructors are creative and flexible in devising writing assignments which will challenge students to think and write about course materials in interesting and meaningful ways.

` c. Instructors are encouraged to use a series of short assignments designed to facilitate critical thinking and writing practice rather than one long one, so that students can improve their writing skills over time. If long papers are assigned, they are to be dealt with in a series of drafts. Common sense and research on the writing process support this recommendation. "W" courses are intended to give students the opportunity to learn to write more effectively and to operate more effectively as scholars as well as to learn specific subject matter. Writing is a skill; writing improvement occurs over time and with continual practice. Short assignments, or multiple drafts, must be responded to so that the student learns what was done well, what was done poorly, and how to improve.

d. "W" course instructors are encouraged to include informal writing activities designed to help students "think on paper" about course concepts. Such activities could include journal writing as well as other generative and structural heuristic writing such as focused free writing, brainstorming/listing, classification, comparison, etc. These writing activities may be short, in-class exercises, and may be ungraded or scanned quickly for content only. Standards of writing proficiency need not be applied to all writing-to-learn activities.

Informal thinking-on-paper exercises (heuristic writing) are important in a "W" course because they emphasize the power of writing to explore, to question, to discover—in short, to help people to think. Of course, such thinking also takes place in the formal writing, but there the finished product tends to be valued more highly than the process of creation. Informal, in-class writing exercises, on the other hand, emphasize writing as a learning skill—a technique to stimulate thought and to try out ideas in a risk-free situation.

"W"course instructors recognize that different types of writing are appropriately evaluated in different ways, depending on how and why they are written. An essay assignment which the student has prepared over time, with opportunity for revision, can and\should be evaluated with standards of minimum proficiency in mind. Standards of minimum proficiency reflect and build on what the academic community expects from students who have satisfactorily completed freshman composition courses (English 101 and 102 or their equivalents). An essay answer written during an exam, when there is neither time nor opportunity for revision, is not evaluated in the same way, particularly in terms of organization and mechanics. Informal personal writing done in class as a learning device is evaluated, if at all, only for content.

e. Both formal and informal writing assignments in "W" courses employ and enlarge critical thinking skills. Critical thinking, within the context of "W" courses, does not refer to some arcane intellectual skill taught only in formal logic classes, but rather to the kind of thinking that college students will be expected to do in all their courses, such as: defining, summarizing, explaining, generalizing, classifying, synthesizing, analyzing, and evaluating. The writing component of a "W" course, then, teaches a student how to employ more than mechanical writing skills, but thinking skills as well.

2. Quality of writing

Since "W" courses are an important part of the total writing program at any college, every piece of formal writing submitted in a "W" course, (Again, formal writing, in this context, means writing which is intended to communicate with a reader, which has been revised, and which meets standards for minimum writing proficiency), should meet the following minimum standards, as appropriate to the course and to the nature of the assignment. These standards reflect and build on the skills studied in English composition courses.

-Clearly stated purpose/main idea/thesis.

-Adequate support/proof/development of main idea.

-Clear and logical organization of information.

-Standard usage of grammar, punctuation, and spelling.

-Standard sentence structure.

-Correct documentation (interior documentation, works cited, and/or bibliography) when required, in a format appropriate to the field.

-Evidence of critical thinking.

The primary consideration in determining "minimum proficiency" should be whether or not the paper communicates clearly and effectively within the context of the assignment, a determination which the instructor must make. While it is important that the definition of "minimum writing proficiency" be understood by all faculty, standards should be adjusted by individual instructors in accordance with the particular demands of their assignment and their field. Faculty are encouraged to publish for students the general writing criteria they expect their assignments to satisfy as well as an evaluation guide which applies to each formal, evaluated assignment. Ideally, such guides would be negotiated between students and professor.

c. "W" course instructors are not directly responsible for the actual teaching of mechanic and usage. Instead, they can refuse to accept papers which are poorly written, requiring students to seek help and then allowing students to revise and resubmit their work.

Assistance should be provided by the college to "W" course instructors and students. Writing centers are often operated by English departments or by academic skills centers. For those students who seem to be unable to produce written assignments that meet minimum standards, writing center personnel are able to help, not only with basic skills problems, but, more importantly, with conceiving, developing, and organizing papers.

3. Grading

a. The writing component in "W" courses is not a separate "add-on" to the normal course content, but rather a series of activities integrated into the normal instruction and evaluation process. Writing is both a way to process information and a way to report the results of thinking. It is as closely connected with course work as reading and thinking are. Students need to realize that the ability to communicate clearly and effectively in their fields is perceived as being essential by the teachers they respect most–those in their programs.

b. The writing component is substantial enough that it would be difficult to pass the course without doing writing that meets minimum standards of proficiency.

Sample Guidelines for Departmental Options

The second method for fulfilling the writing intensive requirement is the departmental option, approved by the appropriate college committees. Usually the departmental option takes the form of a portfolio of student writing. This writing includes several items of written student work–usually five to eight items of formal writing and two to five of informal writing–which represent:

1. The major course work in a department's program of study representing the program's range.

2. The specific rhetorical concerns in a given field of study: for example, lab reports in biology. These items should reflect the minimum standards agreed upon by the given department. The minimum proficiency standards for formal written work in "W" courses should also apply since they are basic standards for the whole academic community.

An example of a portfolio's contents might be:

Social Work Department
Student Portfolio Items to Fulfill the Writing Intensive
Requirement

A. Cover page listing contents and articulating student goals.

B. Formal writing:

1. A case study with analysis.

2. A literature review summarizing and rating ten seminal articles in the field.

3. The written version of a keynote address for a symposium for social workers incorporating ideas, concepts, and theories on individual and family development relevant to social work practice.

4. A periodic assessment of a geriatric or pediatric case.

5. A term paper treating the history of the social work field.

C. Informal writing:

1. A class journal.

2. Field observation notes.
3. Five in-class free writes chosen for submission by the student.
D. A short student self-evaluation.

Portfolio Evaluation

At least two department members should be responsible for the final reading and evaluation of a student portfolio. This reading should take place during the semester prior to graduation before the due date for graduation fees. The full portfolio should receive a pass-fail rating. Departments should articulate an appeal process for students whose portfolios receive a "fail" rating. That process might call for additional or alternate readings and might provide for a limited number of revisions and resubmissions of all or part of a portfolio within specific time period limits.

Faculty Preparation

An intensive faculty development effort is essential both before and during "W" course implementation as well as in preparation for reading departmental option portfolios. Those faculty who are willing to teach writing-emphasis courses normally have a class size of 25 for most "W" courses. As a result, "W" sections are frequently smaller than other sections of the same course when faculty plan courses with chairs.

While many instructors have been assigning writing in their courses for some time, others are just beginning to consider ways to incorporate writing activities. Workshops and training sessions for teachers who are interested in acquiring more facility in using writing to teach should be offered on an ongoing basis. These workshops and training sessions deal with writing as a pedagogical tool, evaluating writing, and integrating writing into curricula. Assistance for "W" course instructors can also be provided through a program of organized opportunities for communication and consultation among faculty using writing to teach.

CHAPTER II

TECHNIQUES FOR USING WRITING TO TEACH

HEURISTIC WRITING

The purpose of this guide is to suggest ways for teachers in all disciplines to use both informal heuristic writing and formal processed writing as ways of teaching. The term "heuristic" is a useful one for such teachers. It is defined in the O.E.D. as an adjective: "serving to find out or discover". (Compact Edition of the Oxford English Dictionary, 1971). Since 1971, the word has also developed as a noun. An "heuristic" has come to mean a set of cognitive moves, a mental procedure recorded and reflected in writing, by the performance of which a thinker/writer/learner can help himself or herself to discover. One might think of all heuristic writing as metaphorical in this sense:

The initial cognitive move of the thinker/writer using any heuristic process is to say, in effect, "I will think of this material or group of materials **as though** it were readily accessible in my conscious mind, or **as though** it were some order, or **as though** it were another thing entirely." In other words, writers consciously superimpose heuristic procedures over subject matter in the service of making discoveries about it. As writers articulate and work out an heuristic procedure in all its parts, they learn about or assimilate or put together the materials in a way that makes them able to understand, order, and then write in a way which demonstrates understanding.

Howard Gardner has recently reminded us in strong terms that our undergirding purpose is to "teach for understanding"(Frames of Mind ,1986). **A central thesis of this book is that the use of writing to teach, particularly the use of heuristic writing, is a prime way of teaching for understanding.**

The 1970's and the 1980's saw the articulation of several "heuristics" by the pioneers who revolutionized the ways Americans think about writing and writing pedagogy. Among these pioneers were Gregory Cowan, Peter Elbow, Kenneth Burke, all of whom articulated heuristics as ways of "tilling the soil of the mind", so to speak–if one could think metaphorically of the mind as ground to be prepared for production. The basis for most of these is "free writing", articulated by Elbow as a means for boosting fluency, though there are more uses for it than that.

These heuristics were originally meant as procedures to be used by writers fo getting themselves started in the writing process, to enable themselves to invent material.

In 1982, Erika Lindemann published her text, *A Rhetoric for Writing Teachers*. On the subject of heuristics, she makes these comments:

> Heuristics derive ultimately from the topoi of classical rhetoric. In Book Two of the Rhetoric, Aristotle discusses twenty-eight "universal topics for enthymemes on all matters," among them arguing from opposites, dividing the subject, exploring various senses of an ambiguous term, examining cause and effect. Although the classical topoi represent lines of reasoning speakers might pursue to invent arguments, heuristics prompt thinking by means of questions. The questions are ordered so that writers can explore the subject systematically and efficiently, but they are also open-ended to stimulate intuition and memory as well as reason (1982, 86).

Though I agree with Dr. Lindemann's comments, this text uses a definition of **heuristic** which is wider than hers as articulated above. Heuristics are more than a "series of questions...ordered so that writers can explore the subject systematically and efficiently." They generate actual learning about a subject as they are performed. The processes involved in what I will call these "generative heuristics" provide a psychic space as well as a means for individuals to both delineate for themselves specific knowledge and fit that knowledge into their own interior construction so that they can use it. The act of writing in a generative heuristic procedure, of being forced to articulate in that way, actually causes learning to happen.

These generative heuristic procedures are quite useful and effective. Several will be presented here in detail so that the reader who wishes to may practice and then adapt them for his/her own classroom assignments.

Among them are two elements which will be particularly attended in this book–Aristotle's topoi or common topics and Gregory Cowan's heuristic called "cubing". An accessible source for the majority of the heuristics is *Writing: Brief Edition* by Elizabeth Cowan. This 1983 edition of the text is an abridged version of the longer *Writing* by Gregory and Elizabeth Cowan. Although Gregory Cowan died early, he was a brilliant thinker about the writing process.

There have been many books on writing across the curriculum since 1965, studies as well as cross-curricular readers, but there have been few which dealt with the ways in which teachers in all disciplines could do it, could use the power of writing as a tool for teaching and learning. *Writing* was written as a textbook for freshman composition with the main concern of teaching writing, but the first section, containing the heuristics, is a major source for people in all disciplines who want to use writing to teach. The need for such a source has become more and more evident.

Aristotle's topoi as listed in *Writing* are these: definition, comparison, relationship, circumstance, and testimony. Now the matter of the topoi their translation into modern language, and their emanations in academia is a matter for a major study. In this volume, there is not room for that study. Suffice it to say that translators of Aristotle's *Rhetoric* generally agree that there are twenty-eight topoi , that they could be characterized as "modes of inference", a term for them coined by William M.A. Grimaldi, S.J. (*Studies in the Philosophy of Aristotle's Rhetoric*. 1972.), and that "the more, however, that one attempts to understand the meaning of these particular and general topics, the more substantial are the difficulties met in the actual statements made by Aristotle in the *Rhetoric*." (1972, 115). It seems that the common topics are still a subject needing further study.

Another thesis for this book is this: what we have called rhetorical patterns or strategies can in fact be usefully regarded as structured heuristics–structured ways of thinking about things in the service of discovery. They are sets of cognitive moves by which we metaphorically perform the initial move cited earlier–to say, in effect, "I will think of this material or group of materials **as though** it were readily accessible in my conscious mind, or **as though** it were some order, or **as though** it were another thing entirely." In other words, thinker/writer/learners consciously superimpose one of these structured heuristic procedures over their subjects in the service of making discoveries about it. As they work these out as structured heuristic procedures, they learn about, or assimilate, or put together the materials in a way that makes them able to understand, order, and then demonstrate understanding in writing. **All students need to possess what**

might be called a personal lexicon of these structured heuristic procedures–a lexicon which they used to have a chance of picking up in freshman composition. These common rhetorical patterns, however, are seldom being taught in any intentional way to students in college. Now they often must pick them up on their own–unless instructors in all disciplines begin to reinforce their use as ways of academic operation.

Students who picked up such a lexicon or set of academic tools could then recognize them as well as exercise them in the rest of their academic operations–if they were astute enough to make the transfers or if a professor had intentionally made them aware of the possibility for such transfers. Students who have at their command such a set of tools that they can consciously use are more efficient academics because these structured heuristics are deeply enculturated in Western academia. They are, of course, under a different guise, the tools of critical thinking. They are the basis, in one or another emanation, for much of academic endeavor. Every time a teacher's pedagogy in any classroom fosters their use, the academic community is served.

Now, this is not to say that the rhetorical heuristics are a panacea of any kind for the ills of academia. If they are used as constrictive forms, then they are as ruinous as freshman composition in formulaic terms was. If, however, everyone in the academic community had an in-common knowledge of them and were adept at their use, then the paths of academic discourse could be smoother. An academic community where students know these heuristics and where teachers can structure assignments employing and containing clue words for them has to produce more satisfactory academic writing for everyone. As well, an in-common knowledge and use of them also would allow the academic community to go beyond them, test and push against their limits, find alternatives. How can we set about finding alternatives when we cannot count on each other's knowledge of the mainstream choices?

Most of the time, these several ways of thinking about things are an unspoken part of the curriculum. Those sharp students who pick up on them usually are much more efficient than their peers. The uncommon student who has been taught them intentionally either as the patterns of academic discourse or as heuristics is an uncommonly efficient one.

In fact, the six generally used rhetorical patterns are so deeply enculturated in Western thought and epistemology that they might be said to be the major paths on which academic discourse travels. Without those discourse paths, discovery and thought is not as easily communicated. In fact, without the use of those patterns as ways of thinking about things, discovery and thought as operations would be seriously hindered.

These basic patterns, as they are explained somewhere in most every book intended as a manual for academic writing are:

1. comparison-contrast
2. definition
3. causal analysis (cause and effect)
4. process analysis
5. analogy
6. classification/division

(Analogy is commonly left out these days. Perhaps it has become too difficult to teach. It is an interesting omission, though, since analogy is extended simile or metaphor...and a primary weapon of pure discovery in theoretical science.)

Be that as it may, a premise of this book is this: **a way all teachers can use writing to foster learning is to use writing as an heuristic exercise, employing these classical ways of operating as heuristics as well as employing the newer heuristic exercises articulated in the 1970's, many of which reflect and/or hook to the topoi.** Later we will discuss using alternate discourse forms such as dialogue which may or may not encompass the topoi research, the structuring of assignments, and evaluation of writing.

These newer heuristics are several. **Free writing** is the basis for most of them. Among many others are **focused free writing, looping, cubing, brainstorming, and webbing/clustering/mind mapping**. Some of these are more structured; some are less structured. All of them offer ways of getting the mind started and/or of inventorying the writer's conscious knowledge about a subject and/or of pushing a writer beyond conscious knowledge to discovery about a subject.

Their uses in teaching subject matter are endless because they offer a way for students to articulate and assimilate their own construction of whatever subject matter is at hand. The products of heuristic writing allow the instructor to gauge the student's true understanding of the subject rather than the student's memorized demonstration of surface knowledge as may be indicated on traditional tests. An aspect of heuristic writing which facilitates that process of gauging is the fact that heuristic writing does not have to be evaluated; instead it can be established as communication between student and teacher. In any working academic's scholarly writing process, again, there is a great deal of writing that is done in the course of things, not for an immediate reward. Much of the prewritng or preparatory writing one does either while preparing an article, a course syllabus, or any document which leaves one's desk is not for an immediate reward such as publication. There is every reason to share that phenomenon with students, to model for them the scholarly process, and to ask that they participate in a like scholarly process. When writing is viewed as a tool rather than as solely a product for use in transactions, then it becomes risk-free and can be used as a way of communicating for other purposes. Whenever specific pieces of writing are evaluated, they should be writing which has gone through the whole writing process. The evaluation should be based on fully articulated expectations from both participants in the transaction...not on the unexamined reactions of a teacher who is the only reader of the writing. Informal heuristic writing has not gone through the whole writing process. Rather, it has started the process or facilitated the process or altered the process or commented on the process.

After all, heuristic writing offers what might be conceptualized as a space in which a person can coordinate the inner and the outer personalities. We all have an inner voice or being which operates all the time free from the influence of society. It is in that inner space where the individual constructs his or her own versions of everything which comes at them in classrooms or in the rest of their lives. It all gets assembled into an individual's whole knowledge system, the one that he or she carries around all the time. That system will contain the fragments of whatever that individual has heard, read, seen...the fragments that the individuals can connect to the rest of what they know. They may be able to insert some specific grouped bits of knowledge about a specific part of a subject long enough to pass a test on them, but the bits that they will take away and remember for the rest of their lives are the ones that they can assimilate into their inner knowledge system. Heuristic writing is conceptually a space where they can do the construction work necessary to assimilate things into their inner knowledge systems. The teacher's ability to share what happens in that space gives him or her what is possibly the most effective evaluation tool of all for every student's knowledge, for that teacher can actually see the assimilation occurring, see what the student knows as opposed to what he or she demonstrates on tests.

Every teacher in every discipline can foster students' use of these academic tools by employing heuristic writing to teach. Both the generative and structural heuristics can be used for informal writing as well as being incorporated into assignments.

Before we review the heuristics, some vitally important general tips about improving student writing are in order. First, here is a list of principles and practice with regard to the use of writing to teach put together by David Schwalm, Provost and Vice President for Academic Affairs at Arizona State University-West:

SEVEN PRINCIPLES OF GOOD TEACHING AND WAC

1. Good practice encourages student-faculty contact.

a. Faculty respond in writing to student writing. With a limited number of concise written comments, faculty can assure students that what they write is valid and important. Always these comments should begin with some positive aspect of student writing and progress to something the teacher as reader needs to better understand the writing.

b. Faculty have individual conferences with students preparing papers. These conferences need not be long, but they should focus on the student text. Communication should concern how the text can be enhanced.

c. Faculty respond to grade concerns. Each assignment should carry a written rubric of traits by which the piece will be evaluated. This rubric must clearly illustrate how a grade will be assigned.

2. **Good practice encourages cooperation among students.**

a. Jigsaw paper assignments. ("jigsaw assignments" are cooperatively produced by students. They might comprise a series with specific students taking responsibility for specific parts of the series. In biology, for example, a group of students could assume the responsibility for the write-ups of a long-term experiment. The final product would then be a compendium of the write-ups.)

b. Peer group editing/invention/critical discussion groups in class. Such groups take a while to bond; students begin feeling responsible to each other only after enough time for the instructor to make clear that the group is the responsible unit. They function best in an atmosphere of shared power in the classroom.

c. Peer tutoring. This is a most effective strategy, but only when students have a little guidance in how to go about it. Checklists for procedure often help. These can be short lists of what to do. For example:

1. Read the writing to be dealt with aloud.

2. Point out the sentence(s) which convey the major point of the piece. If you can't readily point it out, then make one.

3. Name the dominant organization of the piece. (e.g., This is a comparison of...) If it is not obvious, the alter the writing so as to give clue words to make it obvious.

4. Check for the presence of examples to illustrate the major point of the piece.

5. See if you can point out closure in the piece. If it is not there, then construct it.

6. Check the piece for errors.

d. Computer conferencing out of class. This can be done by E-mail on most campuses. Instructors can use macros or red-line editing to inject comments into a piece of writing. Peer conferencing can take place in this way also.

3. **Good practice encourages active learning.**

a. In-class writing to learn in lieu of listening as a catalyst for discussion. Before you begin any discussion, ask students to do a 2-3 minute journal write on your major issue. This could be either a personal reaction or an articulation of what the student needs to have discussed. Through this strategy, each student will have thoughts in order as a preparation for speaking. Also, during a discussion, you can stop for a minute and ask students to write discussion summaries in order to "clear the air". Then the discussion can proceed.

b. In-class writing as a way of bringing closure to discussion. This sort of small summarizing can be invaluable to students when they are studying for tests or other synthesis exercises.

c. Out-of-class writing as a way of promoting maximum time on task and highest order reasoning. Asking students to keep a reading log is a reasonable and valuable way to assure reading gets done. This log can be simply evaluated for length and fullness, not content.

4. **Good practice gives prompt feedback.**

a. Writing offers unique opportunities for "self-provided feedback". (e.g. "That just doesn't sound right.")

b. Peer feedback at every stage. Just as scholars have trusted readers whom they ask for feedback several times during the writing of an article or book, so should students have trusted readers in the context of each class.

c. Instructor feedback within two class periods. Even if it is only one comment, get it on the papers and give them back. Nothing convinces a student that a teacher does not really read more readily than when that teacher keeps a stack of papers for weeks, returning them when their context is long gone.

d. Provide models. Instructors can do their own assignments and share their results with students as models of what they are looking for. They can also share papers done in response to the assignments by students from prior classes. Having a model is valuable for you; it is equally valuable for your students.

5. **Good practice emphasizes time on task.**

a. Nothing encourages more time on task (or better opportunities for clearly defining assignments) than writing. Use of instructional time for in-class writing focuses students on the work at hand, sending the message that writing is a worthwhile use of time. Sharing with students information about the amount of time you spend writing for your classes and for your other scholarly pursuits models to them the amount of time necessary to accomplish scholarly goals.

6. **Good practice communicates high expectations.**

a. Nothing is more challenging to students than writing for you as an audience who is attentive and who will not accept inadequate writing. Also, giving students audiences other than yourself to write for puts you in the position of helping them meet the challenge rather than *being* the challenge.

b. Involvement with other students' writing puts students in an authority role. The ability to help someone improve their writing is one which has to be developed over time; students who see the results of their helping their peers will sooner assume command of their own writing.

7. **Good practice respects diverse ways of learning.**

a. Writing complements cooperative learning and lecture/discussion by placing different demands on students cognitive skills. Asking students both to develop their writing and to help develop the writing of others as well as reinforcing their use of writing as a learning tool–these are superb ways to reinforce the learning processes that make students succeed. These strategies force students to process and assimilate knowledge rather than simply memorizing it.

*This list is an elaboration of the original list of good teaching practices assembled by Arthur Chickering, Zelda Gamson and Louis M. Barsi.

SUGGESTIONS FOR IMPROVING FINAL STUDENT WRITING PRODUCTS

If we want our writing assignments to be learning experiences for students, we need to make sure that the tasks we assign are constructed thoughtfully and carefully. The procedures suggested here will not guarantee that all the papers you get from students will be excellent, but they will guarantee that the papers will be better than ones you would have gotten had you not made that extra effort. Also the time you invest working with students before their projects are completed will pay off when it's time to evaluate the papers. You will already be familiar with each student's work, and will be able to read and respond much faster. More than that, you will have the satisfaction of knowing that you have given students the opportunity to engage in a true learning experience instead of a superficial and frustrating exercise.

CHECK WORK IN PROGRESS

Rather than assigning a paper for a particular date and not seeing it until that time, establish a series of deadlines, one for each stage of the paper, so that you can be sure the students are working. You can then have a chance to identify problems while there is still time for the student to fix them. If you can steer the students in the right direction and help them avoid pitfalls early in the writing process, the whole exercise will be more educational and rewarding for them. There are various methods you can use to look at the students' early work.

A. Collection of Pre-Writing Materials

One way is to collect the students' pre-writing materials: brainstorming lists, proposals, note cards, outlines, rough drafts, or whatever you have asked for, and take them home to skim through. They can be returned, along with your comments, during the next class. The instructor should not feel obligated to do a full evaluation of this early work. Comments about correctness and style are not appropriate at this stage. Concentrate instead on higher order concerns–does the paper have a strong central idea and adequate organization principle? Have the students gathered sufficient data? Do they seem to understand how to use outside sources? If your rapid screening of the papers reveals some students with writing problems that are too serious and time-consuming for you to handle, send them to the your writing center with their papers, your assignment, and your comments, which will guide the center personnel in their work.

B. Student Conferences

Another technique for checking work in progress is conferencing, that is holding brief office conferences with students, either singly or in groups, during which time you look at their work, determine if they are or are not on the right track, and offer suggestions for improvement. This method has the advantages of both immediacy and efficiency. Face-to-face contact with students allows you to assess their degree of understanding and at the same time eliminates the need to collect and carry around stacks of papers. This same method can be used very effectively right in class, if you can clear the time for it. During a single class period, move quickly from student to student, looking at their work and identifying strengths and weaknesses. Whichever of these "early warning" techniques you decide to use, force yourself to read quickly for a total impression of the paper.

The most effective conferencing is that which is not an adversarial situation. If the instructor can begin with one or two positive comments, the conference will be much more effective. The instructor should operate out of this assumption: if the student knew how to write an assignment so as to satisfy the needs of the reader, that student would do so. Thus the instructor can concentrate on the text at hand, help the student imagine a reader, and set about aiding the student in supplying all that such a reader would need. In this way, student and instructor are working on the same side. The instructor can be relentless in urging the student to enlarge the text so as to satisfy such a reader–without alienating the student. Pedagogical ends can thereby be effected rather more efficiently than they can be in a situation where the instructor and the student feel like adversaries.

USE A CHECK SHEET

Ideally, throughout their college studies, students should learn to assess their own writing to develop a sense of what is appropriate in a given writing situation. As we know from our own experience, that kind of sophistication takes years to develop, and we can hardly expect to see much of it in one short semester. The in-progress evaluations described above, however, are one way to encourage that kind of growth in our students. Another way is to provide them with a check sheet for each phase of the writing assignment. Such a sheet would ask students to read their own papers critically, perhaps writing down the main idea, listing the supporting details, summarizing the argument, and naming the sources. If students can't fill out the sheet, that tells them, and you, that they have a problem with the paper. Sample check sheets are Appendix B.

USE PEER GROUPS

Another helpful technique for assessing papers in their rough draft stages and developing students' critical reading skills is the use of peer feedback. Many students have difficulty distancing themselves from their own writing so that they can evaluate it. However, they can work together on others' papers to mutual advantage. Since collaboration is an important technique in almost all professional situations, it makes sense to encourage its use in college. Students can pair up or work in small groups to examine drafts at various stages of completion. Using the technique of peer review has several advantages for student and teacher. First, it turns the whole class into an active workshop; everyone's attention is focused on the writing task. Second, it frees the teacher to concentrate on those students who need extra attention, while other students proceed on their own. Third, it provides students with a live audience for their work.

One reason academic writing is often unsatisfactory is that students feel they are writing only to the teacher, and they know through years of experience that teachers aren't really human. Most of us, as undergraduates, probably wrote papers that we didn't entirely understand ourselves, hoping that somehow, through some miracle, the teacher would. Our students do the same. If part of their task, however, is to make themselves clear to another student, the writing task becomes more realistic. Peer review sessions, of course, must be carefully planned if they are to be truly effective. Students should understand at the outset that they are not expected to "play teacher" or to rip someone else's work to shreds, but rather to respond from their own point of view as a peer.

A written agenda or set of guidelines for each peer review session is essential so that students know exactly what kind of feedback they are expected to provide. The peer review agenda or check sheet should contain concrete questions about the piece of writing being reviewed, questions that identify specific features of the writing that students can look for.

The chart on the following page indicates what kinds of features students can look for in peer review sessions at various stages of the paper's completion. In Appendix B can be found several more sample guidelines for peer review sessions.

PRE-WRITING
Students can interview each other about proposed projects, discuss research strategies, or read each other's proposals.
DRAFT WRITING
Students can read each other's drafts for different traits.
DRAFT 1
Read whole paper for main idea, audience, purpose, major divisions, order of ideas, transitions.
DRAFT 2
Read each paragraph for topic sentences, order of ideas, fullness of development.
DRAFT 3
Read each sentence for syntax, grammar, and emphasis.
FINAL COPY
Students can read again for most important traits and then they can proofread.

SUGGESTIONS FOR UNGRADED WRITING

"If I'm not going to grade it, why assign it?" is a common question from teachers who want to use more writing in their classes, but haven't the time to read and evaluate stacks of papers. The question is logical, yet it presupposes that writing should occur only when we have finished our thinking and learning, that it must be a summative activity to report what has been learned so that it can be graded. We noted earlier, however, that much scholarly writing goes on before submission of a manuscript, writing for no reward or "grade".

In fact, some of the most effective writing assignments you can give are short, informal and ungraded. The extensive section on generative and structural heuristics will provide suggestions for many kinds of ungraded writing assignments. Given a brief time period, usually 3-5 minutes, students write without worrying about correctness (grammar, punctuation, spelling). This frees students from the burden of editing before the material is ready, and allows them to become involved in the discovery process of learning.

The advantages of using ungraded writing assignments are that they actively engage all students in your class, they promote and enhance group discussion, they require little class time, and they do not increase your paper load. These exercises, if used on a regular basis, not only encourage students to come to class prepared, but also can provide valuable insight into the students' grasp of the course material.

1. **Warmup writing**: To assist a class to make a quick transition between whatever else is going on in their lives and the subject matter of the lesson, ask them to write briefly   about what is on their minds and then to put it aside for the remainder of the class.

2. **Speculative Writing**: At the beginning of a class or before a discussion, have students write without stopping for 3-5 minutes on the topic at hand. This can be an important learning   tool to help students think about course content either in generative or structural ways and can establish a personal relationship to a topic that the learning activity begins. For added involvement, have students read their writings aloud, or share in small groups, then synthesize and report to class.

3. **Question Writing**: Ask students to write a given number of questions (3, 10, 25) about something they have just seen/heard/read, or something they are about to see/hear/read. Question writing makes the students confront the material of the lesson more actively and assists them to learn to identify not only what is important about what they have done, but also to identify what they don't know.

4. **Summary Writing**: Students can be asked to summarize a learning experience in one paragraph, or to list the most important points.

5. **Re-focusing Writing**: During a discussion which has become heated or off the track, or between activities in a long class, ask students to write briefly, summarizing or commenting on what has been happening in class. Students can also be asked to list the major points which have been made, to explain the various positions taken, or even to state in their own words a position with which they disagree. This kind of exercise can help students to realize that there can be several legitimate and supportable points of view on a complex issue.

6. **Answer Writing:** Have students respond briefly in writing to a question posed by the instructor. Ask several students, or the whole class, to read their answers aloud; then ask the entire group to answer the question again in writing and compare the results to their first response. Often, without any explicit instruction

from the teacher, students will arrive at new insights by hearing what other students have done.

7. Retrospective Writing: After a lecture, discussion, exam, assignment, or other learning activity, ask students to write freely, summing up the important ideas and their personal reactions to them, making connections with other work done, and identifying questions about the material presented.

8. Generative Heuristic Writing For Problem Solving : This problem-solving activity asks students to write quickly and uncritically, off the tops of their heads, to generate as many solutions to a problem as possible, here and now. Often used by business and industry, generative heuristics encourage creative approaches to problems. The internal editor is turned off during the periods of generative heuristic writing, for some ideas which appear at first to be ridiculous turn out to be brilliant.

9. Structural Heuristic Writing: As they work through a lengthy or complex task or problem, ask students to keep a written record of their ways of thinking about it. The record should include questions, trial ways of approaching the problem–e.g., classification or definition–revised answers, frustrations, etc. This recording technique, while time consuming, provides insight into an individual's problem-solving strategies; in fact, requiring students to formulate questions and answers in writing, actually provides them with a powerful learning strategy.

10. Journal Writing: One of the most effective ways to engage students personally in their course work, journal writing is a long term, continuous written response to learning activities of various kinds. The journal can contain any or all of the non-graded activities mentioned above, as well as class notes, responses to reading assignments or labs, and any thing else the teacher cares to do. Many experts in journal use recommend that the journal be read by the instructor, but graded only according to the quantity of the writing.

USES FOR UNGRADED WRITING ASSIGNMENTS AND RELATED BENEFITS

If a primary objective of non-evaluated writing is to encourage students to write fast, personal, and honest responses, the writing has to be risk-free. In other words, the student should be able to concentrate on his thinking and writing, without having to think about a grade. Students will benefit simply by doing the writing, especially if the writing activity is then used in some way in the class. Some ways to use these writings have been indicated above. Here are a few more:

1. To stimulate discussion: As a preliminary to a class discussion, a brief writing activity can have an amazing effect on the quantity and quality of the response. Because every student has been actively engaged in the topic, through writing about it, more students will be willing and able to respond thoughtfully during the discussion.

2. To sample understanding: Collect a set of summary or   retrospective writings from a class and skim through them briefly to assess the general level of comprehension in the class. There is no need to grade these responses, although you may check them off as completed, if you wish. In a large class, only collect the papers from one or two rows.

3. For review and reinforcement: Collect lists of questions students have about a topic or unit, and base a review session on those questions. Then, redistribute the questions to other students and have them prepare answers. Even later, have students who wrote questions speculate about ways they could find answers to their questions without using the teacher or the text. Have them attempt to answer their own questions and report on the results. This activity has the advantage of acquainting students with resources in their fields, allowing them to practice problem-solving techniques, and fostering their independence.

STRUCTURING FORMAL WRITING ASSIGNMENTS

In using writing to teach, instructors have various purposes for assigning writing. Often, for example, free writing and other generative heuristic activities are used purely as discovery aids for students or as effectiveness indications for teacher use. This sort of writing, in journals or as collected sheets, demands little or no teacher evaluation.

If evaluated writing is appropriate to a teacher's objectives or purposes, then suggestions for that evaluation can be found on pp. .

Responses to student writing–to evaluate or not to evaluate–depend solely on teacher objectives and purposes.

Effective formal written communication is a reasonable goal for college students; assigning writing projects is an important way that teachers can help them attain that goal. Many faculty bravely accept that responsibility by assigning term papers, book reviews, summaries, reports, and essay examinations. Having done so, the conscientious instructor carefully reads all the papers, commenting and correcting, identifying weaknesses, and making suggestions for improvement.

The students, as we have seen a thousand times, generally pick up the graded paper, look at the grade, and either stuff it in their notebooks or toss it in the wastebasket. Worse yet, they may never pick up the paper at all. (Have you ever been reluctant to throw away a student paper, simply because of all the time put into it?) There must be something that we can do to help students communicate better without going through all this futile and frustrating work.

There is, and it has to do with how we handle the student's work as it is turned in. The procedures described here require a little more time initially–there is no question about it–but following them can save you time in the long run, especially those lonely, frustrating hours you used to spend grading the papers. Also, the results will be so much better that you will feel you are really helping students improve their writing, to say nothing of their understanding of the course material.

PLAN ASSIGNMENT OBJECTIVES CAREFULLY

The importance of careful planning, both in framing the assignment and organizing the feedback activities, cannot be emphasized too strongly. If you do not know why you are giving an assignment or are giving it simply because you think students should write a paper in your course, you need to spend some more time evaluating the task. **All the work students do in your classes should help in some way to achieve your course objectives.** What objectives do you want an assignment to achieve? Will it help students master specific course material? Become familiar with standard reference works in the field? Analyze a set of data? Whatever it will help them to do, isolate the subject matter and writing techniques you want the assignment to teach. Appendix A contains excerpts from syllabi created by faculty members on the campus of SUNY College at Buffalo. Look at them to see assignments which address these points.

If you want good results, it is important that you think through, very carefully, what the assignment requires of the student and what the evaluation standards will be. As students, we all struggled from time to time to complete assignments that were vague, ambiguous, or carelessly constructed. Obviously, we want to avoid giving assignments like that to our students. Many instructors find it enlightening, in fact, to do their own assignments before they give them to the students. In this way hidden assumptions and pitfalls are often revealed.

CREATING WRITING ASSIGNMENTS

The problem with poor writing on assignments is that the assignments themselves invite poor writing. Frequently, an instructor gives a student a topic ("Write a paper about acid rain") with little or no direction, sets an expected length and due date, and then waits for the students to submit the paper.

Such assignments, given without backup from the instructor, invite frustration and poorly presented material. What is the purpose of the assignment? What is the student supposed to accomplish? What does the instructor expect? With assignments too broadly or loosely focused, students often create inarticulate prose, not because they have no material or do not know how to write, but simply because they have no clear idea of what direction to take or what to do.

The following is one direction that would be possible to take to devise meaningful assignments:

1. **Set content objectives for learning.** What do you want the students to know or demonstrate with the written assignment?   Good writing grows out of clearly articulated objectives which contain clues for ways students might think about the topic. Objectives might be long and broad, leading to a large research project. A single written assignment for the semester is not the most effective way to use writing–unless that assignment is a semester long sequence involving heuristic writing and several drafts responded to by the teacher. Objectives, on the other hand, might be quite specific, focusing on a single unit and generating a short paper. This latter approach is one that "works" well in writing emphasis courses. It provides the students with more opportunity to clarify what they are learning; it provides the instructor with valuable opportunity to monitor and evaluate the students' progress and to provide useful and meaningful critiques.

2. **Think about the form the writing will take.** Why not consider some "real world" type assignments?   Such assignments might include a letter to the editor, a proposal, a manual, a popular article for a specific publication, a financial report, a newspaper article, a critical review of something, a journal or notebook, a consumer report, a series of annotations of articles, a review of a book.   These forms for assignments lend focus and reality to the writing task.

3. **Consider the intellectual demands of the assignment.** Could you as instructor do the assignment yourself? Are the assignments progressive in degrees of difficulty? Identifying the intellectual demands of the assignment clarifies how the assignment is related to the course objective and assists the instructor in devising methods to best prepare the students for it.

4. **When making an assignment, select an objective, match it with a writing form and create a focused activity.** Here is a brief example of an assignment whose objective was to have students understand the causes of the Civil War:

> Your textbook lists the causes of the Civil War as x, y, and z. Based on your understanding of the war, write a review of that text chapter for Goldenseal magazine, stating the ways in which you agree or disagree with the text. A critical review usually consists of about 3 typed pages.

Here's another:

> Write a detailed letter of the same length to the author of the text expressing your own opinion.

5. **Specify the evaluation criteria for the assignment,** Include a set of specifications for the writing and any other constraints. Set a deadline under which

the students will operate. Students should be aware of what they need to do in order to succeed with the assignment. Criteria also invite questions which, in turn, can further clarify the assignment. Examples of evaluation systems or "rubrics" can be found in the appendices.

Following is an assignment design checklist put together by David Schwalm:

ASSIGNMENT DESIGN CHECKLIST

The Principle of Leverage: All writing assignments should challenge students to the fullest by forcing then to recapitulate key course concepts in economical prose capable of rapid assessment.

Good Writing Assignments:

1. Are short.
2. Are numerous.
3. Require higher order reasoning.
4. Focus on key course concepts.
5. Have more than one right answer and more than one good path to good answers.
6. Stretch students to the fullest without breaking their spirit.
7. Grow out of questions/problems/mysteries/issues vs. "topics".
8. Specify important constraints (audience, purpose) and outline the steps necessary to do the assignment.
9. Designate appropriate points of intervention and offer students opportunities to act on feedback.
10. Offer students clear and realistic models for successful achievement before and after students complete the assignment.
11. Are portable (written down for students).

CHAPTER III

GENERATIVE HEURISTICS

The first chapter contains some discussion about the nature of heuristic writing, setting forth two kinds of heuristics–generative and structural. We can use both of these kinds in our pedagogy for various purposes. The generative heuristics were articulated as ways of pre-writing, but they can be used, as we saw later in the chapter, for many kinds of ungraded writing tasks. These tasks will be used sometimes for the instructor's benefit, as preparation for discussion, evaluation and feedback. They will also benefit the students by allowing them the space to coordinate their individual academic processing as their inner selves assimilate what their outer selves are exposed to. Students should be taught how to do all of the generative heuristics, and then each individual will choose those heuristics which work best for them. Below, five generative heuristics are detailed with instructions for their use. You can teach them easily to students once you understand them yourself, so practice each one in preparation to share them.

FREE WRITING

Free writing is the basic heuristic, and in fact, could be viewed as the model for the rest of heuristic writing. The rules for free writing are simple enough:

1. The writer should be working with a timekeeper of some kind, a silent one. This can be either a person or a kitchen timer or even an alarm clock. The writer's task is to keep a pen or pencil moving on a piece of paper from the point at which that timekeeper says begin to the point at which the timekeeper signals to stop. If the writer gets stuck and cannot think of anything to say, then s/he should write that very thing: "I'm stuck...stuck...stuck. Can't think of anything to write...wish the time were over....this is stupid...". Eventually, the writer will think of something else to write, *and this is possibly the most important time in a free writing period*! More about this later.

2. The free writer should not make any corrections while in the process of writing.

3. The free writer should be assured that what s/he is writing does not have to be shared with anyone unless that provision is made before the free writing has begun.

Later we will examine variations in the free writing heuristic, but now the function and power of this basic heuristic are important. In his book, *Zen and the Art of Motorcycle Maintenance*, Robert Pirsig's subject is the philosophical delineation of "Quality", that most elusive of traits. In the course of the book, he writes about the stereotypical appliance mechanic who comes over to one's house to fix the dryer. This male mechanic goes through his "lexicon" of strategies to make the dryer work. He measures how much electric current is coming through with a little meter. He cleans and tightens all the connections. He does all the things he knows to do to make the dryer run. When none of these work, then he sits and stares at the dryer for as long as five minutes as though to divine its problem. Then he starts to invent a solution which goes beyond all that he knows. In the trade, that is known as jury-rigging. John Ciardi defines jury-rigging as temporary repairs (1980, 215). It seems better defined as high-level cognitive moves producing invention.

This digression has to do with free writing in this way. The initial period of free writing is comparable to the appliance repairman's mentally paging through his lexicon of strategies to use on one's dryer-it inventories all that is readily available in his conscious mind. When the repairman gets stuck and stares, then he is being pushed into the subconscious, the realm of invention or discovery, that place from whence new compositions of knowledge or even new knowledge issues. What he learns on one's dryer, he can then apply to the next dryer he repairs.

Instead, however, of the appliance repairman, here is the free writer having run through all the stuff in her conscious mind and being stuck for something else to say. If she will just go on writing, then something will occur to her from out of that realm of new combinations of knowledge! It may not be profound each time, but there will be times, given the repetition of the exercise of free writing, when there will be a sort of mental "sliding into place" in the mind of the free writer, and she will become engaged in what she is writing. It will suddenly become important to her to get on with this worthwhile thing she is writing. It is most important that teacher/timekeepers repeat the exercise of free writing enough times that each person in their classroom experiences that mental slide. A writer's face will betray that slide, if a teacher is watching. If not, then the teacher/timekeeper will become aware that the body language of the writer is "yelling" her engagement. It is obvious from looking at her that she does not want to stop writing. (So, give her more time! The teacher should be flexible enough to extend the time a bit, but then get on with the day's instruction. It is here that the teacher needs to tout the value of keeping one's free writings in one notebook, because these little writings will become important after a while of regular free writing. They will be the seedlings of future papers.)

The simple exercise of free writing achieves several purposes germane to the academic community as well as purposes germane to specific disciplines. (It is just as effective a tool for the accomplished academic as it is for the student. Remember, the aim is to produce writers in one's discipline who do what scholarly writers do; helping one's own scholarship is an added benefit.) First, free writing boosts the writer's fluency. Just the very simple act of writing under a timed but risk-free situation, on a regular basis, facilitates the writing ability of the writer. Doing it makes her more able to do it! Students who do not have fluency start out writing a few sentences during a five-minute free write. In a very short time, they are writing a page and a half in a five minute free write. Simple fluency is a decided necessity for success in the academic community; therefore, the use of free writing in any specific class is a community service.

Second, free writing gets at the old idea that students "can't seem to get their thoughts down on paper." The timed situation, after a writer becomes trained to it, becomes comparable to a set of switches. The signal to start turns their writing faculty on. The gentle insistence that they keep the pen moving keeps it on, and the signal to stop turns it off. If they are urged to attempt to record whatever comes into their minds during a couple of initial weeks of free writes, then they will begin accruing the ability to "get out of the way" in order to "get their thoughts down on paper". Most writers have to learn to do that. Interestingly enough, professional writers each have some version of the free writing rules that they use when they write. These are their personal writing routines. Hemingway, for example, wrote from 5:00 to 7:00 a.m. every morning standing up at a desk he had custom built. His aim was to produce two usable pages a day, and he had his "switches" so firmly impressed in his own mind and psyche that he could do that most every day. (For more interesting discussions of this, read Annie Dilliard's *The Writing Life*.) Real professional writers do not depend on or give much credence to the romantic idea of inspiration. Working scholars do not either.

Any teacher in the academic community who helps equip and foster student writing is serving the academic community at large, but the service to individual students when one contributes to their scholarly efficiency is at least as important. Boosting fluency and the ability to "get one's thoughts down on paper" certainly will make students better scholars.

The third thing that free writing accomplishes for the individual student is to demonstrate the phenomenon that Lev Vygotsky articulated: "Words engender thought". Students can begin to understand, by their own experience, how human knowledge gets enlarged as one word leads to another and one thought leads to another. Free writing, at the basic, unfocused level, demonstrates this process beyond the slightest doubt. People who spend any time writing have that "mental slide" and find themselves writing things that they did not know were in their minds or that they are discovering at the "point of utterance". Writing has historically been a primary tool of psychotherapy for that very reason; it allows people to distance themselves from their own thought processes and "put things together" so as to save their own lives. It is, again, the space in which one can co-ordinate one's inner and outer beings. Processing in this space, as a tool for learning, has enormous strength. It does in fact allow students to assimilate subject matter into their own knowledge systems; when a teacher shares it, it allows that teacher to monitor the process in a way which is much more revelatory than traditional tests.

The processing which occurs in this space is permanent for the student. Knowledge assimilated in this way becomes a permanent part of students' knowledge systems, added to their interior lexicon of knowledge which they have at hand to apply to diverse situations or to combine in new patterns with pieces of the rest of their systems.

The second rule is also simple but important. Remember that one of our aims here is to facilitate students' being able to get their thoughts to the paper. As every writer knows, indulging the need to correct errors while one is in the process of writing interrupts constantly the flow of one's thinking. It slows down or stops the process, and, even more important, it allows inestimable amounts of what one wants to say to be lost. **In order to work at full capacity as a writer, it is necessary to shut down one's internal editors**.

It is not only the error-correcting internal editor that has to be shut down; it is the internal editor in charge of social acceptability as well as the one in charge of keeping writers on the track of ways of thinking which conform to accepted academic procedures. To work at optimum capacity, writers in the free writing situation must learn not to reject anything that comes to mind. Professional writers are very much aware that they must produce piles of trash from which they or their publisher's editor will then cull the good stuff. In fact, people who work as professional editors have that as their main duty...culling the good stuff from the trash. Once they choose a manuscript to be accepted from among all they receive, then their task is to peel away the trash contained in that manuscript so that it becomes "publishable".

Now the definition of "publishable" is totally relative to particular circumstances. Publishing houses have various goals; among the goals of all of them is a desire to make a profit. They publish books which will sell to a general audience or to a specific audience, but always an audience which will provide enough profit to make publishing worthwhile.

How can we apply this knowledge to using writing to teach/learn? We can give students the opportunities to write under timed circumstances often in our classes so that we foster fluency and get students to see for themselves that writing is a powerful tool for putting it all together in their own individual constructions.

The trouble with assigning an outside journal to students who have not internalized the worth of writing to learn is that they never prioritize writing in it since they do not really see the point. Often, therefore, the writing they do in it becomes another exercise in pleasing the teacher, done shortly before it is due.

Perhaps the most important thing for instructors to remember, then, is that they are **not** obligated to read and/or evaluate everything that a student writes. After all, in the course of working academics' lives, they do a huge amount of writing in preparation or in response or in multitudinous other purposes for which they get no transactional reward. **Students are working academics also; they just generally are not fostered to think of themselves that way.** Instead they think of themselves as receivers or as compliers. A desirable side benefit of using writing to teach is that it contributes to students' ideas of themselves as scholars or academics. Is this not a general service to academia?

We can set up some of in-class circumstances to be totally risk-free so that students are assured that we will not read what they have written. The benefits of being gently forced to write when the only risk is in not writing are inestimable. Students come to see five minutes of writing time at the beginning of a class period as a space where they can say what they want. It may take them a while to begin to perceive that five minutes this way, but once they do, the sense of freedom they feel is awesome.

And what do instructors get in return for giving up five minutes of instructional time to unread writing? The time can be used for the business of class...distributing papers, taking roll, writing assignments or objectives on the board, or distributing papers or handouts. It can also be used to serve teachers' own creativity. These little writing spaces may produce the beginnings of teachers' own papers, as well.

What about voluntary sharing, that is reading aloud of free writes to the rest of the class? Such sharing is usually slow to start, but after awhile. students become enthusiastic about sharing their writing. They cannot wait to get their peers' feedback. Any such reading aloud serves a number of objectives–oral fluency, self-possession, thinking on one's feet, finding errors in one's own writing that emerge when the text is transferred to the oral domain–all these make oral sharing well worth investment of some instructional time. Also, there is always the factor of instructor feedback. As the instructor listens, he or she learns something about his or her effectiveness as well as the quality of student participation.

In the next section, the use of focused free writing will be a matter for discussion, and more teacher benefits from the use of such writing enumerated.
Examples of Student and Instructor Free writing

The following example of student free writing came from a freshman in my composition course. It was done early on in the semester in spring 1992. This is the result of a five-minute time period:

> In my view the masculinity complex most males have is due to the insecurity in their own sexuality. By acting macho they are proving to themselves that they are not gay. They cover up human emotions that could be construed as homosexual thought by acting chauvinistic are cool in front of other people. I myself wear make-up (a woman's thing to do) on a regular basis. Yet I know that I am not gay. I am secure enough in the fact that I am heterosexual, that i don't have to constantly prove myself worthy of being a man. This however does not apply to the people who cry out on the streets "fag", "homo" and other assorted niceties. These people are the ones who are not secure in their role as man. These are the people who at the first sign of a tear cover it up, lest someone think it a homosexual act.
>
> -Aaron Adduci
> BSC student
> Spring, 1992

Aaron was quite a bright person who happened to be into his Mohawk hairdo and his eyeliner. He probably did a lot of thinking about the sorts of experiences his appearance caused. This was a free write that I had specified would be shared with me; we were, however, far along enough in the semester that I had been successful in earning some amount of student trust. Aaron had been doing unshared free writing for three or four weeks.

Late in the semester, Aaron wrote this free write which he voluntarily shared with me. It has the same subject matter for this subject was Aaron's main concern just then. Notice, however, the added length, the widened vocabulary, the quoting from another text, and the widened focus.

This week I read the poem "Big Man, Big M.A.N." by Steve Ignorant of the band,"Crass". It is a poem which tries to point out the utter stupidity of the macho complex many men seem to have.

They are saying [it] is highly due to society and the image men are forced to portray in order to be accepted. For example, "Keep your myth of manhood, it's been going on too long, a history of slaughter is the proof that it is wrong."

They say that because of the myth that you have to act tough to be a man, strut yourself around and the like. Because if your not man enough you won't have the girls , you won't have a good job, you won't get ahead in life. For example, "If you're a man, you'd better act like one, develop your muscles, use your prick like a gun."

They find this theory to be ridiculous and unfair to women. The idea of having to be macho to be a man creates serious problems for women like wife beating, rape and general harassment, and adultery. They state these feelings in this poem..."Slip off in the evenings for a little on the sly, and if the wife complains, ... her first, then black her eye."

They [The band "Crass"] think the whole concept of this is a big joke and that men that act like this are stupid. They think that this attitude causes war and problems for women. And that this is one of the major problems with society.

-Aaron Adduci
BSC Student
Spring, 1992

During the second semester of composition, one of the objectives of the course is to get students to write intertextual papers as a preparation, theoretically, for later scholarly writing. That Aaron should write an intertextual free write is certainly interesting. Actually, an advanced scholar would be quite likely to do intertextual free writing because other texts are the constant corollary discourse of such a scholar's academic operations. Even though the text off which he was working was not a scholarly text, Aaron was getting the message.

Here is an example of a free write by a non-traditional student, an older male who has extensive life experience. Chuck is an articulate person who has always used writing in his professional life as a police officer. At the point of the writing, he had known about free writing for some time, but he had not practiced it.

> I got rooked into this five minute free write by one of the most influential people in my writing history. She is the one who taught me that I can write even though I can't spell, thank god for spell check and computers. I really have no idea what I am doing or what I am supposed to do but she asked for five minutes and five minutes is what she is going to get.

I am sitting here listening to the rain, there is no rain in Arizona where I
live and I am fascinated by how people function in the rain. I wouldn't go
out into the rain if my life depended on it and people here take it for
granted. It is just a fact of life and something not to even consider. The
rain is amazing stuff. It makes everything green and grow, and it keeps the
life going year after year. Still with no rain we have as much in Arizona
as they do here, it's just different.

This key board is at the wrong level and my wrists are already tired.
Must think about getting some type of chair that is adjustable.

It's cloudy and the sky is getting dark and I find that so peaceful. I could
be quite content living here and doing nothing but watching the weather.

This example is not in the context of a course. Chuck is simply an articulate
person who has the capacity to closely record what is on his mind...and these things
were what was in his mind. If he were accustomed to regular free writing, if the
time period had been longer, or if, as we will see later, he were focused on
something, he would have gotten to the "mental slide". He has subject matter, the
weather in Arizona where he lives and the weather in New York where this book
was written. He even has organization as comparison/contrast. Had he continued,
he probably would have targeted specifics as he went, using the comparison/contrast
heuristic to produce more thoughts about aspects of the weather in Arizona and in
New York. Finally, he might have found some engaging aspects of the weathers or
of his personal feelings about them or of his experiences with them to flesh out a
piece of composed writing. However it fell out, he would have learned and
solidified what he perceived about this set of weathers as he went.

Now, experienced writers and scholars know how to use this process, to play
this game with themselves which will allow them to harness their own psyches in
the service of textual production. Teachers who know how to use writing to teach
can do the same thing with their students until those students learn to play the game
independently.

So, free writing is always in the service of fluency. Free writing is never to be
shared unless the fact that is it to be written for sharing is made clear in the
directions. Shared free writing may or may not be evaluated. If it is not evaluated,
it may or may not need to be read by the teacher. In fact, why should a teacher
waste time reading free writing anyway? What could they possibly get out of it?

There are several benefits to reading student free writing. An important benefit
is that reading student free writing is a way to get to know students on a level below
the surface. Particularly when one is teaching large classes, knowing students is

sometimes a difficult proposition. Short pieces of in-class free writing will afford insights into individuals that would otherwise never be available to teachers, will give teachers "handles" by which to connect names and faces. "Oh, yes," a teacher may say. "Tom is the one whose mother just died. He wrote about the funeral." A few of those "handles" go a long way in fostering relationships among students and teachers.

Another invaluable "handle" afforded by free writing is that the teacher can get to know each student as a writer. That makes the possibility of student cheating on any procedure involving writing used in a class highly unlikely. If teachers know how their students write–the vocabulary limits, the turns of phrase, the general sentence lengths, the kinds of writing choices–how could teachers read papers students have *not* written for themselves and be fooled? Another benefit for teachers in reading small shared free writes is that they provide a running, effortless source of feedback for the teacher. If free writing records the thoughts in a writer's conscious mind, and if a writer is free writing at the end of a class period, then the matter of the class should be in the writer's conscious mind. If it is not, consistently not, then the writer is probably not attending to the subject matter in a meaningful way. If no-one in the class records any of the matter of the class, then just perhaps a teacher should re-examine his or her own pedagogy to see why not. This is particularly true if this free writing at the end of class is consistently done over some substantial period of time. In such a case, something is wrong for students are not being engaged by the subject matter of the class enough so that the present thoughts in their minds are connected to it.

Once students are trained in the logistical aspects of free writing and have achieved a modicum of fluency, then teachers can begin to use a variety of variations on free writing which will be discussed in the following sections to serve a variety of purposes.

FOCUSED FREE WRITING

Earlier, the discussion concerned the psychological aspects of free writing as a basic heuristic which allows writers to inventory what is in their conscious minds and push themselves to their subconscious minds where new combinations and configurations of knowledge, individual to them, can be produced. Every teacher can aid in the process of training students in the fullest use of the technique. What about this game the experienced writer plays, though? What version of the game is useful in pedagogy? The teacher takes the position of the conscious writer; the student is what might be termed the unconscious writer. Teachers, by using judicious variations of free writing and connecting those variations with their respective subject matter, can foster students in this process of assimilating the knowledge of the discipline into their individual knowledge systems. Having gotten students adept at the process of recording what is in their conscious minds and pushing themselves to the borders of the subconscious, teachers can then adjust in several meaningful ways.

First, teachers can ask students to FOCUS on a specific topic for a shared free write rather than simply recording their thoughts. Focused free writing has all the benefits of free writing–the "switch" that timing provides, the inventorying of conscious thoughts, the effect of pushing the writer to the edge beyond which discovery lies–but all of them become trained on a specific topic. The teacher who assigns focused free writing asks writers to inventory what is in their conscious minds regarding a specific part of the subject matter of the course. What better way to find out how much students are learning, that is, assimilating into their knowledge systems, about subject matter? The products of a five-minute focused free write at the end of a class period are a most efficient indicator of a teacher's effectiveness in getting across the particular subject matter of the period, a fast way of garnering feedback. Feedback of this kind is both accurate and painless–once the mechanism of the free write is incorporated into the class, and once a relationship of trust is established between student and teacher. Trust in this matter of free writes is as important as any other dimension of pedagogy. If a teacher is not really willing to "listen" to students by reading what they say and responding to it as a discourse of equality, then that teacher will never get the full benefit of using writing to teach. **Using writing to teach means a commitment to fostering student voice.**

Philosophically and politically, the commitment to fostering student voice is possibly the most basic change in pedagogy that a teacher can make. Consider the tradition in academia represented by the kind of writing that students were trained to produce–are still trained to produce in many areas of American schooling.

Academic writing had as its major feature the suppression of the "I". Students were carefully trained to write using "one", "he", "the writer"–words which depersonalized the narrator. It was rather like writing with no hands–or no head! Writers had to go through untold contortions in order to blot themselves out of any academic text they were narrating–as though they were *not* interacting with their subject matter, as though their personalities were not present in the process of assimilation which allows people to write about things. Where did such a tradition ever come from? Philosophically, suppression of the academic "I" was probably done in the name of achieving a scientific stance of objectivity, a reflection of the positivist paradigm in which the ability of an observer to be separate from what is being observed is axiomatic! For the positivist scientist, any hint reflecting influence of the observer invalidates the observation. Academic writers, both humanistic and scientific, were supposed to imitate that stance by blotting themselves out of the process. It was a hallmark of responsible scholarship, one which teachers theoretically were obligated to inculcate into their students.

Politically, though, the effects of this blotting out were to efficiently suppress student voice. Thus, for example, there is a great amount of confusion regarding student research–undergraduate or secondary. The term paper was usually a great lesson in the process of blotting out student voice. The social science teacher who taught American government to seniors had a list of topics that students could choose from. (That was service to student freedom of choice.) These might be topics like abortion or capital punishment. Students picked one of them, went to the library and looked up some encyclopedia articles as well as a few other articles from periodicals, and then wrote a term paper. What resulted was enough to bore the hair off both teacher/reader and student/writer. More importantly, though, what resulted as a process contributed materially to the tradition of student as passive receiver with no voice in his/her own educational life. The term paper was a real representation of the truth of this academic tradition which suppressed voice for it purported to be one thing while it was indeed another.

It purported to be an exercise in learning, in independent scholarship. Had that been the truth of it, then the underlying thesis would have been something like this: "At the beginning of this project, I believed _____ about this topic. Through my reading and talking about it, I have come to believe_____ about this topic. I am going to share with you the story of how I came to change my view including what I read and how I fitted all that together." Through the influence of Ken Macrorie, some secondary schools are in fact making term papers into such exercises, but not many!

Rather, there are still a majority of secondary schools where the list is given, and the thesis statement is made first, e.g. "Capital punishment should be part of the laws of all states." Sometimes the thesis statement is on the list along with the topic. The point is that such a research paper assignment bears no resemblance to real research. In truth, it resembles nothing real. Certainly it is not an exercise aimed at independent scholarship or at the fostering of student voice. Rather, it is a suppression of scholarship since the writer's participation in the learning that even the most simplistic kind of real research brings is discouraged, even suppressed. The writer's voice, asserting an hypothesis or thesis, expressing opinions, or making judgements is throttled if he or she cannot use the "I".

Using techniques such as focused free writing to establish a real discourse between people (teachers and students) who have an equal stake in the particular learning community of a specific class represents a decided philosophical and political shift to what is sometimes known as critical pedagogy. In such a pedagogy, teachers foster student voice without fear of the power such fostering can place in the hands of the student; to foster student voice means to share power.

There are rewards, though, in that shared power means shared responsibility. A teacher who uses writing to teach is interested in the processes of student learning/assimilation. For a student to expose these processes in informal writing, the processes must be happening continuously–that is, the student has to be working and investing in the course on a continuous basis rather than just at memorization time. Else, he or she cannot be recording continuous learning.

Below is a focused free write concerning a mystery novel. It was written by the same adult student, Chuck Leist, whose free write was in the last section. This free write displays a knowledge of the events of the book and provides an assessment of the student's grasp of ways to write about literature. It is longer than his prior free write, since it is focused.

> I have been reading this book called "Mumbo Jumbo" by Kathryn Lasky Knight. The setting is Arizona in the four corners part of the state. The writer brings together real characters that you would find in some of the ghost towns, or semi ghost towns, and makes them real.
>
> The concept of the operation is that there is this underground battle for water–water which in Arizona has started wars and kept the land alive or let it dry up so that everything dies.
>
> A New Age Religion group moves into town and starts buying up all the land to gain the water rights and to take control of the town. The people who have lived there all their lives

are now fighting to save the town and the missing mayor who has been mayor for 50 years.

The story uses settings that we have all found ourselves in and makes them humorous. The language is what we use every day and even though there are some "cuss" words they are used in context and are not offensive in the least.

The final scene in the book involves the heroine's son and the mayor, who is 90, fighting for survival. The book brings out the point that the will toward survival is stronger than the forces of both ends of the age spectrum.

LOOPING

Now, if a teacher were interested in developing Chuck's ability to write about literature, he or she might want to use looping as a way to do that. Looping is a variation of free writing in which writers review their initial free writes and decide on a line or phrase which stands out for some reason or another. Then they take that line or phrase as a focus. They write it at the top of a new page and proceed to do another free write. Usually, the second free write and those ensuing are further developments of the first free write. At some point, if a teacher is interested in fostering development, he will begin to give directive feedback to writers. Here is what Chuck did with his second free write. He chose as his focus phrase: "the heroine's son and the mayor, who is 90, fighting for survival."

The survival of the two is dependent on the 14 year old son being able to do the physical things that the Old Man can't. The mayor drifts in and out of his younger days and comes up with ideas that served him fifty years ago and brings them into the present with the help of the boy. Some of the daring things that the boy accomplishes are dependent on the old man staying in the present time and not drifting along in the past. As each gets more tired and the lack of water affects them it gets harder and harder to keep the old man in the present.

When you add to that the bad guys who are now looking for them in a helicopter, the will to survive becomes the only thing that both the kid and the old man have to keep them alive. How many times did they have the opportunity to give up and say that they can't make it? The will to survive is probably the strongest force in human beings, though it is not brought out until people are forced into situations where it emerges.

Chuck will probably be able to develop the bones of a tight, focused paper from a few more stages of the looping process. It is often a productive process for students.

THE NINE-LINE COMPOSITION

Another variation on free writing is the "nine-line composition". This variation was invented by Margo Figgins of the University of Virginia, who created it. This technique also has an endless number of pedagogical uses. Basically, it fosters coherence because it makes writers connect what they write together. Margo presents it as a language game when she is using it with younger students. This technique has endless applications. Each teacher will want to invent some for his own classroom. These applications can be evaluated for specific purposes or they can be not evaluated, rather simply shared on a voluntary basis.

The rules for the nine-line composition are simple. The teacher should announce that the class members are going to write a paper which will be nine lines long. This takes care of the "How long should it be?" question. In fact, it generally causes a reversal in thinking. Students, instead of wondering how they will come up with enough words, experience the strictures of limited space which make them uncomfortable.

Then the teacher should announce that he or she will give students one word at a time. They should write a sentence using each word as it is given to them. The teacher should say each word and then write it on the board or overhead, unless the exercise is being used as a spelling test.

There are three other rules that need to be announced. One is that the words may be used in any form—for example, the tense may be changed or a gerund/participle form may be used. Another is that margins on each side of the page should be observed. If students are using notebook paper, they can observe the left margin on the front of the page and the right margin which shows through from the back of the page. If they are not using notebook paper, they can draw rough margins on each side. The observation of margins places more strictures on the composition's space, reinforcing the reversal.

The third rule is that punctuation at the ends of the lines should not be placed until the writers see what the next word is going to be, because they might want to continue a sentence beyond the margin in order to accommodate the next word.

Some of these rules are a bit unusual, but each has a purpose in fostering coherence. This exercise works best if the teacher participates, drawing nine lines between margins on the board and writing the composition along with students. She must stress the fact that this is her composition while their compositions should be their own. Perhaps she could define "composition" again for students–the act of combining parts or elements into an artistic whole (Halsey, ed.,1986). As she reads her composition from the board to the class, she should metacognitively talk her way through her thought processes as she assimilated each new word into her composition. This can be a vital part of the modeling processes for reinforcing the structured fluency which makes good academic writers.

The words for the present composition should have been taken from some source–an article, a story, a poem, or a spelling list, perhaps one made up of terms germane to a specific discipline. The teacher should read the original composition in which these words were used after everyone has finished and some sharing has occurred, so that students may see how another author has composed or made his own sense out of the same nine words. That the original author's composition using these words has been published is a fact which might reinforce their ideas of themselves as writers, since they are doing their own sense making out of those same words.

The rule addressing use of different forms of words is quite a useful one. Teachers might require student writers to use varied forms of the words if their purpose were to teach such forms. Demonstration of the intentional use of varied word forms in the process of composition makes students aware of more dimensions in the possibilities for composition.

The rule addressing reservation of punctuation is also aimed at reinforcing the processes of composition. A period or other punctuation at the end of each line shuts down the possibilities for connection to and assimilation of the next element–the essence of composition and, indeed, of the learning process. If one places a period because it is the end of a line, then one automatically looks to forming a new unit with the next word, effectively fragmenting rather than striving for coherence. (The same kind of thing occurs when students writing research papers make up and set down a thesis statement at the beginning of the process, or when they are given one. Automatically, their thesis dictates their research so the process becomes one of supporting the thesis rather than of researching, exploring possibilities and learning. Students should instead be led to formulate a research question in order to give some form to their search. They should be led to understand that both positive and negative answers to a research question are equally powerful in the learning process.)

The nine-line composition is, so to speak, a rendering of the learning process in small. The nine words, chosen and controlled by a teacher, are quite like the array of things that come at a learner in the course of a day. Even when a coherent context is provided by a teacher in a given subject, a learner is constantly selecting from it and rearranging it. Then the learner goes on to the next class and encounters another context with its own array of information. Even though the educational system sends students a message that they must fragment and compartmentalize knowledge into disciplines, individuals' interior selves are constantly striving to make their individual sense of the whole. Using writing to teach in all disciplines is an actualized effort to reinforce the doctrines of critical thinking across the curriculum because it offers a way to transfer and apply knowledge from one place to another across students' whole courses of study. I have used it with second and third graders as a way to test spelling words, and I have also used it to train qualitative researchers for it demonstrates beyond doubt that each of us constructs our own meaning out of all that comes at us. The nine-line composition offers, in small, a representation of efficient learning processes. Use of the traditional patterns of rhetoric as heuristics, which will be discussed in ensuing sections, provides tools for efficiency in the larger learning processes. First, though, several other more recently articulated heuristics will be explored.

BRAINSTORMING/LISTING

Possibly the most commonly used and the most readily accessible heuristic is brainstorming or listing. We are taught to make lists for things long before we go to school. We see our parents making lists for all the operations of living–grocery lists, Christmas lists, "to do" lists–the process of listing things is so basic as to be seldom thought of as a writing function.

The brainstorm variation of listing has become widely disseminated in education as well as in business. The difference between a brainstorm and a grocery list is that the brainstorm courts creativity. It is a list resulting from the push to imagine what might be as well as what is, for it becomes an effort to let "one thing lead to another". In a group brainstorm, minds work off of each other. One person comes up with something and that causes another person to think of another thing. When teachers use the technique as a review process for a section of subject matter, it is a way of setting up the desirable associations out of a group effort which "lets one thing lead to another".

In a group brainstorm, the procedure is to designate a scribe to write on the board, easel, overhead projector, or projected computer screen. Then the group calls out items to be written by the scribe as fast as possible in the order in which they come. Usually, the session will get hot and heavy as "one thing leads to another". As a review process, this is quite valuable to both students and teacher, for the students can supplement their own knowledge with that of the rest of the group, and the teacher will have a definite idea of how effective he or she has been in teaching subject matter by what is readily available to the group.

The addition of two elements to a simple brainstorm session are profitable. The first is the element of timing. A brainstorm which proceeds for a limited time has the same effect as a timed free write–that effect of pushing the mind to inventory all its immediately accessible material and to get on to the edge over which lies the real construction. That same "switch" is thrown that allows concentrated effort and production, the "switch" that allows optimum productivity without the interruption of an internal editor. Whether one is using the brainstorm as an individualized effort to carry on some academic operation or is participating in a group brainstorm, the timing element enhances the effort.

The other element is manipulating the completed brainstorm list by superimposing another operation on it. That further operation is what will be discussed in a later section as the classification/division heuristic. Actually, the qualitative researcher would see this process as content analysis.

After the time is up or the list can be deemed complete by some other means, then the group can be instructed to look at the list for things that are related in some way and can be grouped under some label. These can be designated with numbers or letters so that the list becomes divided into categories. Labels for the groups become an organizational rubric. Depending on the purpose for the session, this rubric could become an organizational structure for a paper or it could become a mnemonic for studying subject matter. If the teacher is functioning as a contributor, then he or she can supply missing subject matter elements as needed.

The brainstorm has endless classroom applications, but the utilization of these two elements boosts its efficiency as well as fostering in students the basic academic operation of classification or categorization.

Here are the results of a group brainstorm from a WAC workshop. The subject was administrators and the aim was to demonstrate how the whole process could efficiently produce the material and organization of a paper.

ADMINISTRATORS

narrow	organized	well-paid
inflexible	necessary	long hours
flexible	responsible	meetings
supportive	tough	unpleasant
no tenure	people skills	demanding
gender specific	skilled writers	duplistic
attend to detail	designate well	maintain calm
have ulcers	friendly	distanced

This list is abbreviated from the original, but it serves the purpose. Then next step is to categorize the list by using numbering to indicate like things.

ADMINISTRATORS

narrow (1)	organized (2)	well-paid (3)
inflexible (1)	necessary (3)	long hours(3)
flexible (2)	responsible (2)	meetings (3)
supportive (2)	tough (1)	unpleasant (1)
no tenure (2)	people skills (2)	demanding (1)
gender specific	skilled writers (2)	duplistic (1)
attend to detail (2)	designate well (3)	maintain calm (2)
have ulcers (1)	friendly (2)	distanced (1)

We put (1) beside what we called "The Bad", (2) beside"The Good", and (3) beside "The Ugly". The category names, of course, designated negative, positive, and "other" characteristics, from our viewpoint. The last category was mixed since it contained characteristics which were necessary but could be good or bad depending on the identity of the observer and the context. For example, while it is true that a good administrator must be able to "designate well", often the person who is designated ends up with an extra, undesired task. Also, administrators work "long hours', often much longer hours on campus than faculty do, but then administrators are better paid than faculty. "The Ugly" became a relative category.

It was quickly obvious to this group of participants that a paper could be efficiently produced out of this brainstorm list.

CLUSTERING/WEBBING/MIND-MAPPING

Gabrielle Lusser Rico in *Writing the Natural Way* (1978) articulated an heuristic which she called clustering. The method was taken up and later renamed "webbing". A variation of it made its way into the domain of cognitive psychology where it was called "mind-mapping" or "cognitive mapping". The process remained much the same wherever it emanated. It is viewed by some (e.g., Lindemann) as a visual representation of the brainstorming process. One version of this heuristic gets at categories during the initial process . Clustering functions as a highly efficient generative heuristic for some writers/thinkers/learners.

Clustering is a visual representation of cognitive moves. The writer/thinker/learner starts with a blank sheet of paper. In the middle of that sheet, he or she places the subject at hand. Then he or she proceeds in one of two ways:

1. In a set amount of time, using the same "switch" effect that timing has on any of the generative heuristics, all the associations in the conscious mind are recorded by means of words written on lines drawn in radiation from the circled center subject. No one association is followed to its end at this initial session; instead one simply records all the associated words. Then in a second consideration of this initial map, any associations which seem engaging to the writer receive further exploration. This further exploration might be performed with a second map where the initial association is mentally pushed until it ceases to be productive. The product is a visual representation of the mental processing dealing with the subject in a way which effects that same push that comes from effective free writing, the push to the end of conscious knowledge on a subject and on past that end into the subconscious realm of discovery.

2. The other version of the process is one which uses the same mechanism of timing, but which attempts to follow out initial associations on the spot until their productivity is exhausted. This version effectively limits the number of associations but also effectively widens them out.

Clustering can be employed at any stage of the learning/writing process. It could be used, for example, to begin the study of a new area of course work in order to inventory for teacher and student the amount of knowledge which already exists concerning the subject matter. It could be used as a review tool, to represent the associations that teaching has effected in the minds of individual students or as a group undertaking to reinforce those associations for the whole class. It can be used in the initial stages of thinking for term projects or at any stage of the writing process involved in them.

CHAPTER IV

STRUCTURAL HEURISTICS

Earlier in this book, rhetorical patterns used as heuristics was discussed. The six structural heuristics discussed below-definition, process analysis, comparison/contrast, causal analysis, analogy, and classification-are renditions of the topoi generally used in western thought in their true function as structured ways of thinking about subject matter. The cubing heuristic, a combination of all in a quick and dirty operation, is the last structural heuristic discussed. Every professor needs to teach and re-teach the structural heuristics as ways of operating for academic efficiency, using them in assignments as directed ways for students to proceed, depending on how you want them to learn about a subject. It is always essential for a teacher who is writing assignments to define terms so that both the teacher and the students have the same notion of what these terms mean. It is not enough to say, "Compare..." or "Classify...". Instead the teacher must explain what he means by these procedures and must be *sure* that students understand. When that is done, any teacher will get better products from writing assignments-and will foster students' general academic operating abilities, their independent scholarship.

DEFINITION

The structural heuristic of definition is a process which dominates the time of most academics. Actually, definition is what dominates the time of lawyers, doctors, and executives in their professional capacities as well. In the specific rhetorics of each discipline, as teachers are requiring their students to observe formats, conventions, and specialized forms, definition is embedded in all the intellectual proceedings. If teachers will intentionalize their inclusion of specific definition in their assignments as well as their classroom modeling, their own as well as their students' efficiency with this particular process will be enhanced.

How does one define? In the same way that lexicographers define, though most often thinker/writer/learners want extended definitions rather than short ones. The short ones are probably harder to write. One of the features of the intentional short ones are probably harder to write. One of the features of the intentional process of definition is that it often reveals surprising things about words. How often we look things up in dictionaries and find that they mean not at all what we thought they did or that they mean much more than we thought they did. When thinkers/writers/learners have the structural heuristic of definition as one of their cognitive tools, their use of language comes to have much greater width and depth.

The cognitive moves involved in classic definition are these:

1. First one mentally places the object to be defined–be it idea, concept, construct, place, or physical thing–into the largest class to which it can be said to belong. That part of the process is sometimes revealing. For example, if one were defining "desk", then one could place it in the class "furniture" without much difficulty. However, if one were defining "property", some thinking about its largest class might go from attempts to articulate property as "things" or "land" or "houses" to articulating property as a man-made construct, in fact a concept which is particularly a trait of civilization.

2. Second, one has to cite the essential qualities of the object to be defined which delineate it from all the rest of the members in that largest class. Here is where definition becomes most specifically a process in the service of discovery, for ascertaining and naming essential qualities of the object to be defined means learning about it in the most intimate way. What is the essential quality of "desk"-ness? Why is my dining room table often a desk? Why is my bed sometimes a desk? Why can I recognize an elegant white and gold table with curved legs and carved edges as a desk equally as well as I can recognize a large metal construction with drawers and a "modesty shield" as a desk? Probably the essential quality of a desk is that it has a surface which is clearly intended as a place on which to write or which the user arranges as a place on which to write.

The ability to work the process of perceiving and naming essential defining qualities as a way of thinking about things is a highly facilitative skill for thinker/writer/learners both in their academic and in their personal lives. Clarissa Pinkola Estes in *Women Who Run With the Wolves* (1992) continually warns women of the necessity to "sniff out the real natures of things and people" in order to make wise choices and protect their souls. She spends many pages of text talking about naivete as a paralyzing aspect of womens' psyches, about "wide-awakeness" as its opposing quality. If a woman or person is wide-awake to her own psychic predators or to predatory behavior from the people she encounters, she can make wise choices for her life and her childrens' lives. If not, if she cannot perceive and name the essence, the real qualities of her own psychic workings or of the people she encounters, she is doomed to unwise choices often disastrous to her own life or her childrens'.

In defining "property", once one has it in its proper place as a construct of man, then one can see that its essential quality is the idea of ownership. People can own houses, cars, clothes, other people, boundaries, ideas, words, religions, patents...the property construct in fact pervades civilized behavior. It is the primary pretext for war. It is a crucial issue in personal relationships like marriage or the parent-child relationship. It is a motive for the highest accomplishments of man. It is an important ingredient in the debate between "nationalism" and a world governmental organization. It is a basis for the workings of politics on all levels.

A discussion about respective definitions and ideas about property is one every couple contemplating a long-term relationship ought to have. Perhaps every person contemplating a long-term contract with an institution would profit from investigating institutional policy with regard to the property concept, also.

In academic terms, this process of defining is entirely necessary for efficient learning in all disciplines. Teachers can use timed writings focused on this structural heuristic in connection with important disciplinary materials to evaluate students' deep understanding of specific subject matter. They can make assignments of varying sizes involving definition as well as modeling it in the process of daily teaching. The procedure of naming class and essential features is one of the most useful structural heuristics. Teachers' metacognition in using the heuristic themselves is very important for student learning.

Essential features can be communicated by enumerating examples of the thing, by articulating characteristics of it, or by citing applications of it as well as in a myriad of other ways that will be invented by the individual instructor. Here is an assignment fostering use of the definition heuristic:

CRJ 203
Dr. Blank, Instructor

Block Watch Associations often have among their members one who volunteers to be a "designated victim" in matters of disturbance of the peace such as might be a consequence of uncontrolled parties, "keggers", which have recently been a source of problems in major cities. Discuss the need for a "designated victim" in matters of this kind, defining that term as well as defining the term "crime". Show in your answer the importance of such definitions in police proceedings.

Evaluation Rubric:
An "A" answer to this question should contain:
1. Content:

a. Extended definitions of the two cited terms, definitions which employ the classic method of placing them in their largest classes and then demonstrating the difference between them and the other members of their classes.

b. Material demonstrating the need for these terms in police proceedings.

2. Organization:

a. Clear connection of the answer to the question.

b. Evident definition, connected to the requested background material from the field of criminal justice.

3. Surface features:

a. Neatness.

b. Adequate and sensitive paragraphing.

c. Correct spelling of all terms from the criminal justice field; few errors in other spelling or usage errors.

A "B" answer could vary from the "A" answer in these ways:

1. Content:

a. Less thorough definitions of the terms.

2. Organization:

a. Less clear definitions.

3. Surface features:

a. Errors in paragraphing.

A "C" answer could further vary in these ways:

1. Content:

a. Correct use of terms, but inadequate definitions.

2. Organization:

a. Weak connection to background material.

3. Surface features:

a. Some spelling errors.

b. Less neatness.

Remember, be careful and thorough in processing your definitions and in connecting them to the background of the field!

PROCESS ANALYSIS

Writing about a process is simple enough, isn't it? That is what everybody seems to think when they assign essay questions which deal with processes. Then when they are reading student papers, too often they find slapdash renderings which jump around and leave out numerous steps of the process. That is when the muttering about how students can't write starts again...

In composition classes, often I have made simple process assignments like "How to Make a Peanut Butter Sandwich" and then have brought materials to class which would allow us to follow the directions for such sandwiches. The debacles which took place in those classes were wonderful! People left out the bread, the knives, the jelly, the spreading...these enactments certainly gave the lie to the belief that envisioning and writing about a process is simple.

Modeling and articulating process as an heuristic is a vitally important task for teachers in every discipline. In an earlier section, I suggested using process as a tool in the analogical heuristic, but straightening it out as an heuristic in itself is in order, also.

Generally, a process can be thought of in three stages: preparation, implementation, and clean-up. These, too, can be metaphorical, but usually they are descriptions of actuality. One plans for and assembles needed materials, whether tangible or intangible. Then one implements a procedure step by step from beginning to end. Last, one replaces materials and records closure or clean-up. The process falls into a mental shape which makes it understandable to the observer or reader.

In the center, the implementation process can be in any of several kinds of order. It can be a chronology with time as the organizing principle. It can be an example of spatial order which starts at a physical point and proceeds from point "A" to point "B" and perhaps back again if that is necessary. It can be an example of discrimination where the thinker/writer/learner has prioritized from what is most important to what is least important and leads the reader through that priority list. I can be an example of order from general to specific or from specific to general. The important thing is that there be an easily discernible order and that the thinker/writer/learner be apprized that it is important not leave out any steps. This means he or she must get down close to the process and look for detail. Perhaps it might be useful for teachers to remind students to think like writers who must get their characters from place to place in the course of moving a plot along. Another strategy for them might be to think like parents who have to tell offspring how to do something like tying shoes.

This "getting down close" in order to be able to enumerate steps is rather a profitable undertaking for both teachers and students. We live in a society which discourages our "getting down close" to anything. Our lives speed by us in flashes. Advertisers purposely interfere with our thinking process by timing commercials so that they leave a quick impression not able to be examined and re-examined. We provide ourselves with schedules which leave us breathless at the end of each day. In schooling particularly we have been devoted to the instant response–in spite of what John Dewey told us about the delayed response so many years ago. The idea of close examination in the service of discovery is undoubtedly one of the most valuable ideas that teachers can give to students. Articulation of a step by step process so that a reader is able to follow it is an activity which embodies close examination. It is an heuristic which furthers in a trenchant way the attempt to educate for understanding rather than for coverage (Gardner, 1986). It is an heuristic whose importance must not be denigrated in any discipline for it is as basic an academic operation as is definition or comparison.

Consider this example of an assignment which intentionally employs process analysis.

BUS 201: Business Communications
Instructor: John Sterling

Assignment: Orientation Directions

Tom George has been an employee of Andersen Consulting for one year. At this point in his career with Andersen, he must begin presenting proposals to prospective clients. You are his immediate supervisor, and you have to get him ready for the tasks ahead. Write a set of directions for Tom. In this document, you should address step-by-step the procedures for contacting a client, drafting a proposal for a specific project, preparing the proposal for presentation, and doing the presentation. Write the document in memorandum format. It will probably be about four pages long. This assignment is due in final form at the class meeting six weeks from today. You could begin the process of writing this assignment by doing a brainstorm which you could categorize into a tentative paper plan. Your first draft must be brought in to class for peer conferencing two weeks from today. Your second draft must be brought to a conference with your instructor four weeks from today.

CLASSIFICATION/DIVISION

The rhetorical pattern of classification/division used to be defined as a pattern in which the writer took a large group and divided into smaller groups by some guiding principle. Then the writer labeled and wrote about the small groups. The teacher of composition usually superimposed a five-paragraph pattern over this one, and student papers emerged which looked like this:

Paragraph 1: Introduction which characterized the large group in general and in which the last sentence stated three names of small groups.

Paragraphs 2,3,4: Individual discussions of the three groups with examples of each.

Paragraph 5: A conclusion which restated the introduction and made some general remarks about the groups.

Neat little packages were these little themes. Mostly, the composition teacher corrected the errors on those themes and handed them back to the student with a grade. A liberal composition professor allowed students to correct their errors and resubmit the paper for a better grade. Seldom was there much discourse between student and professor. What discourse there might have been did not often concern the power of classification as an heuristic...but then that was long ago in another day of composition teaching, was it not? Things have changed now, have they not?

Classification is another of the Aristotelian topoi which have become the undergirding methodologies, the heuristics of Western learning. It is another structured way of thinking/writing/learning about things. When a writer articulates a classification process effectively, it emanates like any of the other topoi as an overt, easily apprehendable organizational pattern in a piece of writing. So how might the matter of classification as an heuristic be handled as part of the discourse of any classroom across the curriculum? Perhaps it might be helpful to think about where classification is particularly prized as an heuristic. In the discipline of biology is one place. Might not one safely say that the epistemology of that whole discipline has been dominated by the classification heuristic, for biologists have traditionally operated as scholars by dividing large groups into smaller ones according to some guiding principle, which often emanated as a set of common characteristics marking a class.

In every discipline, however, classification is a powerful scholarly tool. Let us redefine classification as a heuristic. Classification is a way of thinking/writing/learning about things which has this structure. First, the thinker/writer/learner perceives some boundaries around a large group of things. Sometimes those boundaries are preset because they are given by an instructor (e.g., Families in various societies or in various levels of one society might be a large group under discussion in an "Introduction to Sociology" class) or because a group of things has some predominant characteristics which mark them as being alike (e.g., female administrators) or because they all happened in the same time frame (e.g., the events surrounding a crime)–or for any one of a million other reasons. Sometimes they are boundaries set by the thinker out of need or individual perceptions. For example, my dissertation was a qualitative one in which I interviewed people who had gone to and/or taught in one-room schools. When I came down to actually doing it, I had to set some boundaries or I could have gone on forever interviewing disparate people whose only commonality was their experience on one-room schools. I decided on a geographical boundary, interviewing people who lived in one rural Virginia county and who had that common experience. When I had done the interviews and had the tape transcriptions from them, I had to perform another of those classification heuristics with the materials, devising groups. At this point in the process, I called it content analysis, but in reality, it was only an application of that classification heuristic.

I have a student, though, who has some money to buy entertainment equipment. He has used classification to set up groups out of his own perceived needs. One of the boundaries is the amount of money that he can afford. That boundary limits his large group somewhat, but within those limits he has set up these groups: stereos made up of components from various companies, stereo sets from individual companies, and TV-stereo combinations. He is using the classification process to help him make a consumer decision.

Once a large group is defined, then the writer looks for a guiding principle by which to make smaller groups. This step in the heuristic process is the hard one. One way to proceed is simply to begin with a random member of the large group and examine it carefully, perhaps brainstorming about it in order to enumerate its characteristics. Then examine another member of the large group to see if it is like the first in any way. This is a slow and painstaking process, but it is one in which deep learning takes place. If teachers want students to use pure discovery and to experience a profound form of independent scholarship, they may set up situations in the course of a semester where students are set to such empirical tasks, with plenty of free writing or one of the other heuristic variations at each step of the way, and a formal paper growing out of them at the end of the process. Perhaps one of the lab reports in any chemistry class needs to result from the classification heuristic; perhaps a full semester project producing a formal paper at the end of the course might involve a classification of all the lab experiments done in a chemistry course.

So what, again, is the concept of the "guiding principle" for classification? It is what might be called a facilitating commonality. For example, we might take the large group "Christians in America" and divide them by any number of guiding principles. The most logical and most obvious is denomination. If we use denomination as our guiding principle, then we have Methodists, Baptists, Lutherans, Catholics, Christian Scientists, and so on. We could, though, use types of doctrines as our guiding principle and come up with groups like those who believe in some form of predestination and those who believe in free will. We might use degrees of fundamentalism as our guiding principle or we might use degree of likeness to the original forms of Christianity. The possibilities are unlimited, but the point is that each group can be divided and characterized in the light of this facilitating commonality. Dividing spiders into groups by the numbers of legs they have is a widely known facilitating commonality.

Another example might be the group "people who come to a college campus in the course of a day". This group could be classified according to their sex, but it might be more productive to classify them according to the function that they fulfill on campus. Then they could be grouped as students, administrators, faculty, clerical workers, janitorial workers. Each group could be discussed in terms of their characteristics if a student were writing a formal paper, after the student had done some informal writing in the process of clarifying thinking about such a large group.

It seems self-evident that every time a teacher in any discipline asks students to practice classification as an heuristic process, writing about it either formally or informally, the academic community profits. Not only are students being reinforced in their fluency, but they are being required to articulate their personal practice of an heuristic process that is another powerful learning tool for all disciplines, one that should be a part of their individual lexicons of such tools.

Now, how can individual instructors inject writing which fosters this practice into their pedagogy? By learning to structure subject matter assignments which require such practice. Generally, they need to review as well as to model the classification process with students, but students who have had composition instruction (Composition is defined as the act of combining parts or elements in order to form an artistic whole...) aimed at fostering their competence in the deep conventions of academic discourse will be familiar in some degree with the process. It is, however, dangerous for instructors to make assumptions about such student knowledge. Perhaps students have not had a composition course for some time and have not been asked to practice the skills learned there since or have never been asked to practice them in any context but a composition course. Perhaps, even though it is unlikely, they had composition instruction aimed only at the level of error or in other stylistic directions.

Instructors who use writing to teach in writing intensive courses are not responsible for correcting error unless they so choose, but they are responsible for reinforcing heuristic rhetorical tools for learning. All of them do not need to be attended to in every course of study, but each course of study can and must attend to some. The instructor can choose whether and which to attend through the requirement of student writing.

How then can an instructor inject the classification heuristic into his subject matter assignments in an intentional way? By structuring assignments so as to require articulated practice of the classification process. Here is an example from a professor of political science:

PSC 326 Politics and the Media
Dr. Rom Desai, Inst.
TOPIC: WHY WOULD I HAVE SUPPORTED BUSH, CLINTON OR
PEROT FOR THE PRESIDENCY IN 1992?

A Word or Two about the Assignment:

Fall 1992 was a presidential election year. Especially for those of us who are involved in studying the media, that year promised to be a very exciting year for a variety of reasons:

a. Our country was no longer facing external threats from our long time opponent the former Soviet Union. Consequently, the communist bogeyman was not an issue in this year election.

b. The L.A. Riots demonstrated rather graphically on television screens that if the economic and racial problems go unresolved, we face crisis situation at home.

c. The entry of Ross Perot, the Texas billionaire, as a third party candidate interested a large number of our citizens. They seemed to think they had an alternative that year, consequently, they did not remain as indifferent and apathetic as they had been in the past.

You will be reading and listening to a lot of the 1992 media presentations about these candidates. The assignment calls for selecting and writing an essay on any one of the candidates you prefer and for trying to establish reasons from your exploration of the media current in 1992 for Clinton's victory.

The following suggestions will be helpful in preparing your assignment:

Step One:
A brief overview of the book by Arthur Biddle and Keilnetli Holland, *Writer's guide- political science*, (Lexington, Mass: D.C.Heath Co. 1987), will greatly assist you in the preparation of this assignment.
Step Two:
Before you begin writing the assignment you may want to ask:
A. What do the newspapers, news magazines, prime time news, various documentaries shown on the television tell us about Bush, Clinton and Perot?
B. What do I want to know about the presidential candidates? What do I already know about them? How and where can I find out more about them? Do they conjure up anything unusual? Is this important to me?, meaning does this interest me? Can I experience this in writing?

C. Identification of specific focus: Try to sort your observations-(findings) into categories-such as personal, family, position on various issues- political, economic, social etc. Try to know what specific questions you want to examine in your assignment and as you proceed try to identify trouble spots. As humans, we respond to our experiences, when taken together, such responses constitute a view of the world. What are the reasons for your preference for say, Bush or Perot? What impresses you most about your candidate? Can you say something about his style, character, leadership etc.? Why do speculate that Clinton won?

Step Three:

Prepare an tentative "jotted" outline of the essay before writing it. This will greatly facilitate the structure and the organization of the essay. You will quickly notice the "missing ingredients". This in turn will add balance to the essay. You will be able to discern what needs to be added and what needs to be left out. As you proceed, you will be making more detailed outlines.

How to Structure an Answer to this assignment:

A. Citation: On the top of the page give the assignment full citation: Why Do I support Clinton or Perot?

B. Introduction: The first few sentences usually are the most important. Try to introduce the general topic of the assignment in first few sentences. Try in a way that you should impress the reader with why the subject matter is vital; try to sustain the interest of the reader. Sometimes you can begin with an anecdote or a brief statement about the experience you have had that might also interest the reader. The introduction is usually an over view of the position you are taking in the paper.

C. The Body of the Paper: The first several paragraphs after the introduction should discuss the most important point of the assignment. It should be the strongest, supporting your point of view. Do not concern yourself with objectivity. Value judgements are inherent at this

point.

1. Identify problems: For example, deficits, collapsing infrastructures-both social and physical, health care, unemployment, decline in manufacturing etc..

2. Articulate ways to show the weaknesses of the candidates you do not support.

3. Show why the change is necessary-- some comparisons.

4. Strength and weakness of your candidate

5. Refute opposition arguments.

6. Conclusion.

Miscellaneous Writing-Tips
   A paper receives higher score to the extent that it demonstrates the following.
Consider:
      A. Can the same thing be said differently–in fewer words maybe.
      B. Do your words exactly convey what you have in mind?.
      C. Can this be expressed more eloquently?.
      D. Remove ambiguity-(if not intended).
      E Does the essay stray at some point from dealing with the central idea?.
      F. Does the information selected, manipulated and presented advance the
purpose of the paper?.
      G. How well do you justify the data used?
      H. How well you articulate your arguments?
      I. Is it possible to improve the essay?.
      J. Is there any paragraph too long or too short?.
      K. Is the grammar and spelling correct?.   Read and re-read, with an
analytical and critical mind to see if the essay can be improved keeping the above
features in mind.
Requirements for this paper.
   It should be typed, double-spaced, and should not exceed twelve pages.
Fifteen references is about the minimum acceptable number.
   The deadline for submitting the paper is October –, at the conclusion of the
class. Consequences for missing the deadline–ten points will be subtracted for
each day missed. Please pay attention to surface features such as neatness,   clarity,
and organization. Should you have any question during the process of your writing,
please feel free to contact the instructor.

COMPARISON/CONTRAST

   Another rhetorical pattern to consider as an heuristic is comparison/contrast.
Possibly, comparison /contrast is the most common way we have of
thinking/writing/learning about things, but it seems we have a "muddy" idea of this
process as an heuristic. Most learners do not know whether to view comparison and
contrast as one process or two discrete ones. The process of comparison is the same
as the process of contrast–one mentally or physically sets two entities belonging to
the same large class in proximity to each other. Then one observes/thinks/writes
about them to find out whether they are alike or different from each other. Carrying
out this heuristic process is highly revelatory for the observer/thinker, for it helps
immensely his or her capacity to see the essential nature of both members in the
pair. If "X" is true of "A" member of the pair, then is it true of "B" member? If
not, then what is true of "B" member? When the observation process is articulated
and composed into a paper recording it, both the learner/thinker/writer's

effectiveness and the nature of each member of the pair can be revealed. (Obviously, comparison/contrast can serve definition, also.)

The process gets labeled "comparison" or "contrast" as an end label. If one finds the members of a pair to be different in a majority of ways, then he or she has a contrasted pair. If they reveal themselves as alike in a majority of ways, then the label is comparison. Always, when one is writing about comparison/contrast in academic endeavor, one must acknowledge both likenesses and differences, concentrating the bulk in a written presentation of this heuristic process on whichever is in the majority.

It has been said that too much of Western thinking is based on the process as it is labeled contrast. Sometimes it seems that we have the need to see black opposing it in order to see white. We often perceive in terms of dichotomies--good vs. evil, love vs. hate, illness vs. wellness--and we seldom include a middle term. Opposition is much more convenient, much easier to think about than less well defined areas--like grey or indifference or chronic illness that one provides for while one otherwise lives a "well" existence. Often one of the results of the comparison/contrast heuristic is to reveal the existence of a middle term or ground between two entities which was not before obvious.

On the other hand, we are pleased when we can compare one entity to another and see likenesses. We learn quickly when we can find a likeness in a new thing to something we already know. In fact, we are probably enculturated to respond favorably to likeness, to look for and to celebrate like qualities. Americans basically want the rest of the world to be like America. We are just now making a cultural effort to accept and celebrate difference, but we are still not near the point that we can refrain from trying to turn difference into likeness or that we have an easy time tolerating the "third term", that is entities who have or adopt some traits of likeness to us but retain some traits of difference.

Perhaps it is useful here to point out the fact that the words "compare" and "contrast" are used about as loosely as is the word "love". Quite often, when we say we are comparing, we are really contrasting or we are really setting up competition or at least discrimination and value judgement. When we say that one thing "compares well" with another, what we really mean is that one thing is as good as or better than another. The rhetorical heuristic of comparison/contrast is not a way of thinking about things which generically involves competition, unless the area of value judgement is added as a last step in it. A responsible teacher understands the reality of what s/he is doing when s/he equips students with all of these ways of thinking/writing/learning about things. To help students understand and perceive comparison /contrast as well as the other traditional rhetorical patterns as heuristic operations (structured ways of thinking about things) and to help students acquire the power of choice to separate the processes from their associated enculturations is a political act, one as powerful as fostering student voice. These things are the tools of critical thinking. Critical thinkers do not accept anything without trying to perceive the truth of it, and so they make very efficient citizens.

So, now, how do teachers inject the processes of comparison/contrast as an heuristic into their pedagogy? First, it behooves them to understand in an intentional way how it works.

In order that they may be effectively compared or contrasted with one another, first two objects, ideas, concepts or whatever must be posited as separate entities whose traits can be enumerated. Initially, they have to be defined. (Quite often, remember, one rhetorical heuristic serves another. The perception of that truth is one reason rhetorical modes went out of fashion as a major component in teaching freshman composition. Teachers began to feel that presenting them as discrete patterns, with a paper to be written in each pattern, was unrealistic. They were right. The only problem was that instead of shifting to view them as a lexicon of heuristics, ways to think, write, and learn about things, many composition teachers abandoned them completely. "Babies and bathwater...".)

They must have discernible boundaries between them, e.g., I can compare my behavior now in connection with some specific person to my behavior in the past with regard to the same person. Time would be a discernible boundary between these behaviors. That same boundary would apply to war in history.

Then the things must belong, at some place in the roles/traits that can be attributed to them, to the same large class. If they do not belong to the same class at some level, then we cannot compare or contrast them. Consider the old saying that one cannot compare apples and oranges. One can certainly set up to compare them for both are kinds of fruit. They are such different kinds of fruit, though, that one is forced to contrast them, instead. Now, one can neither compare nor contrast apples and hedgehogs, though a clever writer might analogize them most effectively. Analogy will be discussed in the following chapter.

This heuristic process is pretty overt if we are contrasting, say, high school and college life, but if we are comparing/contrasting intangibles we may have a bit more complication. For example, love and hate are both emotions, easily compared or contrasted because they are clearly bounded from each other ("...opposite sides of a coin"). Indifference and tolerance are a much less clear pair, though, tending to overlap. Clear initial definition for purposes of the comparison would be necessary if the heuristic process were to be efficient with those two.

Now, learners need to understand the power of all the heuristics through clear, simple application practice. Comparison/contrast, like the other heuristics, best works when it is practiced in the simplest, most unprejudiced fashion possible. The fewer preconceived notions held by the thinker/writer/learner, the higher the efficiency level of the heuristic. The writing which results from its effective practice should be equally clear if it is a faithful record whose purpose is to lead the reader through the process. The writer needs to remember that he or she is not communicating with a mind reader, so that each step of the way must be articulated. The teacher/reader needs to remember that also. Given the achievement of fluency on the part of a writer, writing coming out of the comparison/contrast heuristic should reveal to a teacher the truth of students learning processes.

Following is a look at how the lab report, a piece of formal writing, can become an extended use of writing to teach. This plan for the lab report fosters fluency and requires articulation of the comparison/contrast process, using theory and practice in the boundaries of a given experiment as the pair undergoing observation.

WRITING FOR LAB REPORTS
Composing the Results and Conclusions Section:

In the Results and Conclusions section of your report, you will provide three types of information: a brief account of what you did during the experiment, an explanation of the results, and a comparison between results and theoretical predictions. In comparing the two, you will demonstrate your understanding of scientific principles by explaining what caused the discrepancies you observed. You are not yet writing the section itself; you are carrying out a pre-writing activity. The order in which you generate the material isn't important. You needn't worry yet about grammar, punctuation, spelling, etc., and it doesn't matter whether or not your are writing in complete sentences (you will pay close attention to these matters toward the end of the writing process). Look over what you have written. Did anything else of importance occur during the experiment? If the answer is "yes," jot down the important points you left out. Have you included details that aren't important? If so, cross out what you don't need. As you compose this section of your report, you may find the following steps useful:

1. Pre-writing about results. Write in response to the following questions: What procedures did you follow in conducting the experiment? What were the results? What problems did you encounter? How is this like other experiments you have performed in this class?

2. Prewriting about theory. Forget for the moment what actually did happen and consider what in theory should have happened. Without being concerned about organization or mechanics, write the important features of the theory.

3. Comparing theory with practice. As another pre-writing activity, write in response to the following questions: How did the results differ from the theory? In responding, refer to your pre-writing about theory. What could have caused the discrepancies between theory and results?

4. Writing a draft of the section. Sum up what you wrote about theory as concisely as you can, and next do the same for what you wrote about results. Then

account for discrepancies; what might have caused them? Although you need not arrange the material to fit a predetermined form, you need to include somewhere an account of what you did, an explanation of the results, and a comparison of results and theoretical predictions. You will probably write three or four paragraphs, one each for procedures, results, theory, and observations (a comparison of results and theory with a discussion in which you will account for discrepancies). Writers often choose to combine procedures and results in a single paragraph. Your first sentence might be a statement that concisely explains the extent to which results and theory do and don't correspond. Another alternative is to begin with a brief statement about what you did. Regardless of how you begin, you must present your material in a logical sequence. At the end, you will discuss possible reasons for discrepancies between theory and results; be sure to take into account any variables not covered by the theory. For instance, you might say, "The predicted standard deviation was 2.5. Results differed by 2%." Then you would account for the difference. The last part of the section may be the most interesting to write since it provides an opportunity for you to demonstrate your understanding of the principles governing the experiment.

5. Revising. Ask yourself, Have I left out anything important? If you did, expand the draft to include the needed material. Next ask, What can I take out? Get rid of unimportant material (for example, needless explanation of routine procedural steps). Is the structure of the draft sound, or do you need to re-arrange some of the sentences so they will flow in a smooth, easy-to-follow, logical sequence? Change the order of the sentences where appropriate, and add transitional words as needed: for example, "then," "next," "in addition," "however," etc.

6. Editing. Before completing the revised version of the section, check the mechanics: Are there incomplete sentences? If so, get rid of them by turning them into complete sentences or incorporating the fragments with ideas you expressed in other sentences. Are there errors in grammar, spelling, punctuation? If so, correct them. These types of errors are aesthetic flaws which mar the attractiveness of your product. More important, if there are many such errors, they will detract from the clarity of your writing; the errors will distract your reader from what you are saying as he/she struggles to determine the meaning. (If you compose your reports on a computer, you may find spell-check or "grammatik" helpful.) NOTE: Generally people writing in English prefer the active voice because it is thought to be more direct and vivid than passive. In technical writing, however, writers use the passive voice for stylistic reasons; you must make certain your writing conforms to that convention. Examples:

ACTIVE: I inserted the disk in the A drive of the computer.

PASSIVE: The disk was inserted in the A drive of the computer.

Composing The Summary

You should prepare the "Results and Conclusions Section" before you write the summary even though you will place the summary first in your finished report. In writing the summary, you will condense the material from the Conclusions section to provide a concise, factual account of what happened during the experiment. The summary will include a brief statement of the procedures you followed and a description of the results (i.e., the data collected). In other words, you will provide in the summary the same information, in abbreviated form, that you did in the Conclusions section except that you will not include your own opinion; the only time you should give your opinion in the summary is at the end, where you should provide a brief statement that the results of the experiment do or don't agree with the theoretical predictions.

1. Writing a draft of your summary. You can draw upon the revised "Results and Conclusions Section" in writing the summary by identifying the most important points about procedures, results and theoretical predictions. Your summary might begin with a brief statement of the procedures you followed, or your first statement might suggest the theoretical predictions for your experiment, as in this example: "The efficiency of a centrifugal impeller is related to the blade discharge angle." Regardless of the approach chosen, you will discuss procedures, results and theory. Your discussion of each will be brief; for example, you may have written an entire paragraph in the Conclusions section about procedures and results, but you will need only a sentence about each for the summary. The discussion of procedures should be a brief explanation of the kind of data you collected not a step-by-step account of what you did, nor a repetition of material from the procedures handout provided by the instructor. A good way to end the summary is with a brief statement about the extent to which the results agree with the theory; for example, you might say that the data collected "agree substantially" with theoretical predictions. You won't provide details about how closely the results and the theory agree, however, nor will you discuss the reasons for discrepancies.

2. Revising the summary. This step is the same as for "Revising the Results and Conclusions Section" above. Note: Since the summary should be as concise as possible, it is especially important to get rid of inessential details during revision.

3. Editing the summary. This step is the same as for "Editing the Results and Conclusions Section" above. After following all these steps, your product should be a tight paper suitable for submission.

ANALOGY

Analogy, another structural heuristic, is a specialized form of comparison–between two entities which are *not* of the same class. Another name for it is metaphor. Earlier, the observation was made that analogy as a rhetorical form has all but disappeared from freshman composition readers and writing manuals.

That is hard to understand, because analogy is an enormously powerful rhetorical heuristic. Consider this article which came from *THE TEACHING PROFESSOR* (7:5. May, 1993.) though it was adapted there from the newsletter of the Association for General and Liberal Studies. (11:3. December, 1992.)

In Praise of Analogy

by Don Foran, Centralia College (WA)

Critical thinking, multiculturalism, and assessment are important buzzwords in contemporary education circles. They are all worthy subjects for inquiry. What teacher does not want his or her students to do more than regurgitate only what has been ingested from lectures, assimilated from dominant-culture socialization, or experienced but not-evaluated?

I am convinced, after 20 years of inveterate metaphor peddling, that helping students acquire the ability to think analogically may be the most important general education work I do.

For at least a dozen years now I have capitalized on the quirky aspect of my own personality that impels me to look at one thing and see another. My English composition students know, for instance, that their task is to keep the reader "on board." They have been fruitfully thrown off balance themselves, for example, by magicians doing card tricks. So I've suggested that in writing, as in card tricks, "those who control the mechanisms control the results."

In literature and philosophy classes, contemporary applications of perennial classics, like Antigone, Billy Budd, and The Plague emerge, with a little prodding, with metaphorical, analogical intensity. Albert Camus, for instance, probably meant The Plague as a not-so-subtle exploration of Nazi-era pestilence, but the novel clearly has implications for the era of AIDS and all manner of political and social inertia. After exposing my beginning composition students to traditional modes of expository writing--Description, Definition, Observation/Inference, and Cause and Effect--and a healthy diet of revising, I introduce my favorite: Analogy.

I relish digging out those compositions from quarters past that inventively explore a shadow subject with which a student is familiar, in order to reveal the real subject, generally less familiar, more abstract.

Current students delight in a composition written six years ago, "The Bite", which suggests that the vampire bat ("the name

given to certain bats which attack humans and other
warm-blooded animals and drink their blood") has more than a
little in common with the I.R.S., which also can't be warded off
with garlic and crucifix. They gasp as "the vibrating ionic
movement" of ants, taken collectively, is compared to human
intelligence. ("If such things exist, they can have nothing to do
with us," dryly comments the writer.)
Bullfighters are shadow subjects for essays on social activists
(who are rewarded not with ears but with passage of a better
health care bill). Carpentry, with which a student may be quite
familiar, is used to explain far different forms of craftsmanship,
like writing analogy compositions.
I believe that all writing is an opportunity for better thinking.
Analogy is a particularly enriching opportunity to communicate
the unfamiliar by means of the familiar. The richer the
experience, the vocabulary, and the imagination of the student,
the fresher the writing, the more powerful the creation. I would
argue that analogical thinking is a quintessential learning tool.
For example, one student compared Picasso's art to making
salad. When a student has successfully grappled with
communicating a subject as complex as cubism, when she has
grasped the power that resides in words that interest, even
surprise, another learner, our task as educator is almost
finished. The student has become a teacher.

- Adapted and reprinted with permission from
Association for General and Liberal Studies,
Newsletter, 11:3, December 1992.

One cannot help but note the differences between his list of "traditional modes of expository writing" and this book's list of rhetorical patterns used as heuristics. Perhaps is it time that this murky and almost taboo subject of the traditional patterns receives some attention from more than just a few of us. Perhaps the practitioners in the field need to spend some meeting time on this subject.

Don Foran is an English teacher, but he is one who realizes the power of analogy/metaphor as a "quintessential learning tool". This power has long been recognized by the new science. Thomas Kuhns records that. Gary Zukav does, too, in his wonderful book about physics, *The Dancing Wu Li Masters*. The superb analogy in the title sets the scene for "an overview of the new physics".

Most well-known examples of the products yielded by use of the analogic heuristic in thinking/writing/learning are in the established lore of fields. The field of medicine is notable, of course, for its use of analogy. (e.g., Langerhan's islands). So are space science and computer science (e.g., condoms against viruses which destroy information on disk, resuscitation of crashed computers.)

There are some other literary techniques which are specialized forms of analogy. In poetry, analogy is called metaphor. Metaphor and simile are both poetic terms for comparison, but they are different in degree of power. Similes compare with the use of "like" or "as"; metaphors leave out the "like" or "as", simply calling one thing another by way of establishing the comparison. (e.g.,"Your eyes are like pools of clear water" is a simile, but "...the eyes are windows to the soul." Similes are illustrative, attractive, effective, but metaphors have more power to comment.) Long poems which work out metaphors in all their points of likeness are called extended metaphors or "conceits", just as long pieces of prose which work out such comparisons in all their points of likeness are called analogies.

Analogy and metaphor/simile are specialized kinds of comparison (not contrast) between two things which are *not*, on any level of role or trait, members of the same class. (Apples and hedgehogs rather than apples and oranges.) At least in the mind of the writer, though, this unlikely pair display a few outstanding qualities in common, seen as a result of thinking analogically or metaphorically. There is a section on the SAT of one word analogies where one has to name the relationship between the first pair in order to see the same relationship between another pair.

For thinker/writer/learners, articulating those likenesses in detail, once they have been perceived, is a revelatory process. The revelations ordinarily concern both members of the pair, once the analogy has been fully worked out. In fact, the process of analogy so often causes the thinker/writer/learner to "see things with new eyes" or in fact to "see" things which do not *yet* exist, that it is a most powerful tool for the production of new knowledge. Is that not what the inventor does? "Sees" things which do not yet exist and then creates those things? We tend to regard inventors as being gifted people whose natural talent gets expressed in new products, but we do not put a high enough value on the inventor's facility at analogic thinking...and articulation.

The point becomes, though, that every learner ought to be able to think/write analogically or metaphorically. It is not a natural gift limited to inventors, poets, or talented writers. How can teachers across the curriculum use analogic thinking/writing to teach?

Basic elements in getting students to think and write analogically are the teacher's giving them permission to do so and the teacher's modeling of the process. In WAC workshops, using analogy as a heuristic is possibly the hardest process for participants to make their own. Perhaps the reason for this lies in the fact that analogical thinking requires freeing the mind from conventional patterns, and it requires a conscious refusal on the part of the thinker to reject anything coming to mind while one is practicing this heuristic. Free writing and webbing contribute to these capacities since writers who practice them learn to turn off their "internal editors" and to record whatever comes. Webbing, particularly, can produce the basis for an analogy. The intentional practice of the analogical heuristic, though, improves and expands ones ability to use this "quintessential tool of learning".

Teachers can model analogical thinking constantly in the way they choose to present material. Often the connection that makes students able to learn difficult concepts is an analogical one yoking something familiar with the new, difficult concept. Robert Fulghum's book, *Everything I Need to Know I Learned in Kindergarten*, is a prime example of this kind of teaching. Whether or not one likes that book, it has appealed to huge numbers of people who find edification in the way Fulghum yoked together the simple precepts taught in kindergarten with the large and serious problems encountered in adult life.

A current example of analogical teaching in teacher preparation on the pedagogy and evaluation of writing is the analogy of the writing teacher and the coach. (Other examples of current analogical thinking in education are the "teacher as manager" analogy basic in William Glasser's work on "quality schools", and the whole idea of education as business which has begun to become reality.) There is an aphorism which states that when the metaphors/analogies change, the world changes. If one believes that language generates reality, then one almost has to agree with that premise.

This is how the analogy between the writing teacher and the coach works out. The writing teacher, especially the freshman composition teacher, used to be conceived of as a person who gave some direct instruction about spelling, usage, and mechanics of the American language as well as about rhetorical patterns and then made assignments for papers to be written by students and read by the teacher. In a clear transaction, [Another piece of analogical thinking on the part of James Britton (197?) is the view he articulated in which he analogized the process of school writing to giving and being paid for something, transaction. The writing is compared to a product for sale and the price for it a grade in terms of this analogy.], the student gave the writing to the teacher and the teacher gave back a payoff–a grade. The transaction ended there so that teaching writing was a product oriented undertaking.

The new composition theory and resulting pedagogy posits the writing teacher in an entirely different way, as a coach. (The teacher-coach analogy is beginning to spread across the curriculum and people who use writing to teach across the curriculum are in the forefront of that spread.) Now, the coach prepares his team to interact in a competitive situation with another team...not with himself. The team plays another team in front of an audience. When they are out on the field playing, the team members are on their own or at most loosely connected with their coach. They are using the coach's preparation in order to function independently. A most important feature of the relationship is that the players and the coach are aligned together to face an audience or an opponent. The coach is *not* that audience or opponent. The coach teaches the rules of the game, the forms of competition, and specific techniques...and then he sends his team members out to play by themselves.

After writing teachers or any other teachers consciously work out this analogy, then if they buy into it, they must radically change their idea of what teaching is. Teachers who become coaches have to abdicate their positions as sole receivers and judges of their students' products.

Rather, their relationships with students get entirely redefined. They and the students are aligned together to prepare the student for the playing field–two against the world. Teachers' roles start being perceived as having different components; providing the figurative playing field gets to be paramount. *Teachers begin spending their pedagogical energies in constructing situations where students can become aware of their own needs to know–rather than spending their energies in telling students what they will need to know for a test.* Such situations need to have components which will demand that students learn what the teacher wants them to know so that the course of study's objectives are met. Then the teacher can do the direct instruction needed, but now such direct instruction is in the service of students' self-perceived needs. For example, if students are writing articles to be sent to the local village newspaper, then they need to be able to get these articles in as error-free shape as possible. They will need to know how to use quotation marks if their articles contain quotes from interviews, and they will need to know some interview techniques in order to do those interviews. The teacher's who is acting as the coach helping students accomplish goals to prepare for this "playing field" is an entirely different person from the teacher who is assigning papers or material with the sole purpose of his or her own evaluation in mind.

One sociology professor who uses writing to teach sends his students out to the malls in the city where his campus is located. Their purpose there is to survey mall goers on some topic which they have proposed as their semester project. They must write their own surveys and must have rudimentary knowledge of the techniques involved in experiential research in order to carry out this semester project, and then he asks that they get their project reports in shape to submit for publication. He has to help them to do that, of course, providing them with whatever they need in order to complete the project and thereby assuring himself that they have learned what he had set for them to learn as objectives in the particular course of study.

This look at the power for change exercised by one product of analogical thinking underlines the importance of teachers across the curriculum giving students some practice in using analogy as a heuristic. This is, as Dan Foran says, a "quintessential learning tool".

So teachers constantly model the process, yoking together new concepts with familiar ones–as they coach their students– and, by modeling, they give students the idea of analogical thinking, but it is also necessary to inject opportunities for analogical thinking/writing/learning into pedagogy.

Here is an example of a specialized analogical heuristic called the "tagmemic heuristic". In its original form, it was invented by Richard Young, Alton Becker, and Kenneth Pike. Published in their text, *Rhetoric: Discovery and Change* (1970), it allows the systematic examination of a subject from several perspectives. (Later, this text will examine Gregory Cowan's "cubing" which gets the same effect through free writing.) Young, Becker, and Pike maintain that any subject can be analogically/metaphorically viewed from three perspectives. Their example is an oak tree which people usually view as an isolated entity–a thing or "particle". But we could also view the oak tree as a process or "wave" for it is part of the growth process that begins with an acorn and ends with lumber. Again, we could view it as a "field" or system in itself of roots, trunk, branches, and leaves.

Also, for Young, Becker, and Pike we must be able to figure out three aspects of existence for the oak tree–or for any other subject we are viewing through the tagmemic heuristic. One is what makes it unique–as a particle, wave, or field. Another is how much it can change and still be itself–as a particle, wave, or field. The third is how it fits into the larger systems of which it is a part–as a particle, wave, or field.

Thus the learner can use these six concepts–particle, wave, field, contrast, variation, and distribution– to produce a nine-cell chart often referred to as a "tagmemic grid" or "matrix". (Young, Becker, Pike, 127).

W. Ross Winterowd has a simplified version of the tagmemic in *Contemporary Rhetoric*. (1975, 94). He uses the Los Angeles freeway system as a subject. He views it:

1. As an isolated entity and describes its physical features in great detail.

2. As one among many of its class and explores how it differs from the rest of its class.

3. As part of a larger system and describes how it integrates with the other highway systems.

4. As a process rather than a static entity and explores the continual changes in the system.

5. As a system rather than an entity and describes the parts of the system and how they fit together.

Assignments, formal or informal, which demand practice of these highly structured, specialized manifestations of analogical heuristics in any class are ways to foster analogical thinking. Once instructors begin to invent assignments which employ the analogical heuristic, though, they soon go beyond set systems, letting their own professional perceptions aid their creativity.

Anything can be thought about, for example, as an ecology...

One specific kind of analogical heuristic was articulated by the great rhetorician, Kenneth Burke, in *A Grammar of Motives* (1969. p. XV). Burke is essentially a philosopher, but his work is valuable to the entire academic community inasmuch as it concerns the whole problem of language. Burke views rhetoric as including all of the "symbolic means of inducing cooperation in beings that by nature respond to symbols" (*A Grammar of Motives*, 43).

Burke's "pentad" is an analogical approach to subject matter which posits subject matter as drama, always involving *motive* and *motivation*. His method allows the user to look at any subject as a collection of variables which can be metaphorically viewed as these five things–act, scene, agent, agency, and purpose–in order to examine things as action and ends.

In a rounded statement about motives, you must have some word that names the act (names what took place, in thought or deed), and another that names the scene (the background of the act, the situation in which it occurred); also you must indicate what person or kind of person (agent) performed the act,, what means or instruments he used (agency), and the purpose. Men may violently disagree about the purpose behind a given act, or about the character of the person who did it, or why he did it, or in what kind of situation he acted; or they may even insist upon totally different words to name the act itself. But be that as it may, any complete statement about motives will offer some kind of answers to these five questions: what was done (act), when or where it was done (scene), who did it (agent), how he did it (agency) and why (purpose). (*A Grammar of Motives*, p.15).

In *A Rhetoric of Motives*, Burke broadens the scope of rhetorical theory. He argues that rhetoric uses symbols as a means whereby human beings act out with each other the drama of life. (Perhaps it would be useful to enlarge "human beings" to include personifications when one uses the pentad as a tool for analysis in subject areas outside the humanities.) The dramatistic pentad as an analogical heuristic can be used to learn about historical events, current events, literary or biographical subjects, or scientific processes most effectively. When thinker/writer/learners can say "*it is as though*" this subject were a drama in itself, then they can reveal much to themselves about the subject. Here is an assignment from the field of economics which asks students to use Burke's pentad as an analogical heuristic:

ECON 314 - Economic Theory
Dr. Susan Davis, Inst.

Write a paper in which you use Burke's pentad as a tool to analyze John Stuart Mill's theory of utilitarianism.   Remember that you will use Burke's five terms–actor, act, scene, agency, and purpose–to write about Mill's theory as though its story were a drama.

Start by free writing for 5 minutes, allowing your imagination to be free, on each element of the pentad and Mill's utilitarian theory.

The resulting paper should be about five pages in length. It should be divided into sections, each titled with one of the parts involved in the pentad.

Your purpose here is to see what you can discover about Mill and about utilitarianism by thinking analogically about them.

Following is another analogical assignment, this time in math.

MATH 341
Linnear Algebra

The use of linnear algebra might be compared to the skill of bull riding practiced in the American West. Consider these likenesses between the two:

1. Both are difficult, demanding a high skill level.

2. Both are not directly practical, though each is a part of more practical skill applications.

3. Both take a certain amount of courage and willingness to face danger.

4. Both demand a knowledge of direction and ability to gauge it closely.

5. As an exercise, both demand close timing.

6. Both have specific sets of moves–one cognitive, one physical.

Though this seems an unlikely comparison, it enables one to see a new perspective on both members of the pair. Using a cluster with linnear algebra in the center, see what comparisons you can come up with. Don't reject anything that comes to your mind. Instead, write down any comparisons that occur to you, and then pick a one to match with linnear algebra and work out the comparison.

Then write it into a paper of about two pages. Give examples for each step of the comparison, devoting a paragraph to each.

CAUSAL ANALYSIS

The last of the structural heuristics to be considered here is perhaps the most important, perhaps the least important. It depends on who is thinking about it.

Post-positivism as articulated by such people as Lincoln and Guba, (1986), redefines the concepts of cause and effect, pointing out the impossibility of separating them.

This heuristic honors post-positivism, actually, for it fosters the ability to "see" things in this way: The student can posit an event, an idea, a place, or a thing as cause *or* as effect. One is reminded of a lawyer who defends a divorced husband against the petition by his former wife that the court raise his child support payments in the morning court session. Then he represents a divorced wife for the same sort of petition against another husband in the afternoon court session. He is working with the same set of circumstances from the completely opposing position; cause and effect get reversed.

In the world of academic operations, this ability to understand and to manipulate causality is a necessary one. As in any other heuristic, the thinker/writer/learner is forced to "get down close" to the subject, but in working with "sliding" causality, he or she is also forced to create mental metaphorical reality for the purposes of the task at hand–to be able to say "*it is as though*" this thing is cause and "*it is as though*" this thing is effect and to explore the resulting relationships through writing. This capacity to envision and explore causalities is one necessary for higher math operations, for medical research as well as medical diagnosis–actually, for most higher cognitive undertakings.

In writing from this heuristic, the thinker/writer/learner can by describing his or her subject, characterizing it as whichever–cause or effect. Then the writing can explore the effects or causes related to it. In making assignments employing causal analysis, teachers can specify the need for identification of primary and secondary causes/effects. Such assignments would have to follow class discussion and modeling of the processes by which one can separate the two, which will vary with the discipline. (Certainly those processes might be different in botany class and in philosophy class.)

For example, suppose the class was journalism and the subject for writing were a train wreck. The assignment might describe the facts of the event:

> In Springfield, Illinois, on June 6, 1974, there was a train wreck which happened in a suburban area which had grown up surrounding train tracks. These tracks had relatively little traffic. Much of the train traffic which used them was not during business hours. Crossing the tracks was a road leading off of a major route which it intersected to a shopping center popular with the townspeople. Along this road there was a liquor store, a Farm Bureau supply store and a post office. The tracks were built on a slight rise so that the immediate land on either side was ditch-like. Adjacent to the tracks, the depression fell away from the road providing almost no shoulder and approximately a two foot drop.

One fine spring day, and elderly gentleman who was a cautious driver had been to the shopping center. He proceeded to drive his car out of the center, along the road, across the railroad tracks and on out to the major highway where he stopped to look both ways. He suffered a mild stroke while waiting to enter the highway, so he did not move even though automobile traffic began to line up behind him. Back in the line behind, there was a rig pulling a gas tanker which was positioned partially on the train tracks. When a train approached at a train's usual rapid pace, the tanker had nowhere to go to get out of the traffic line, so the train, unable to stop in time, hit the tanker broadside.

The resulting explosion was great. It produced a wall of flame which rolled back to the liquor store, causing an explosion there also. Seventeen people, including the tanker driver, were killed that day. Property and cars were destroyed. It was a terrible disaster which produced insurance investigations and court cases lasting many years afterward.

The elderly gentleman was, of course, unhurt. He subsequently recovered from his mild stroke and lived on for several years.

Write a news story in which you treat this wreck as a cause. Explore five of the direct effects of the wreck such as the loss of property. Then explore two secondary effects such as the state senate seat left empty by the death of the senator who was in the liquor store buying a fifth of expensive rum with state funds.

or

Write a news story in which you treat this wreck as an effect. Explore three direct causes of the wreck such as the train engineer's failure to stop in time. Then explore three secondary causes such as the inefficiency of the road building which left no shoulder or other means of getting out of a traffic line.

The heuristic process of articulating cause/effect relationships is useful in every discipline. Consider this assignment employing causal analysis:

America seems continually to be waging a "War on Drugs" or a "War on Poverty" or a "War on Crime" and lately, a "War on Terrorism". Choosing one of these as an example, write about the waging of this sort of war as a cause rather than an effect. What are the ramifications when we wage one of these wars? Are there economic ramifications? Are people's lives affected, especially those of law enforcement officers, of law-abiding people, of criminals?

THE CUBING HEURISTIC

Last under the discussions of structural heuristics is a technique invented by Gregory Cowan. It is what is known in the education business as "quick and dirty", meaning that is it a surface exploration rather than one that is in any depth. Cubing functions as a quick and efficient way of ascertaining the approach to a subject which is most productive to the individual writer. It is not one of the topoi; instead it is a short compendium of them. According to what may very well be an apocryphal story, Cowan was sitting in his office at Texas A & M with his feet up on his desk, thinking about writing. His eye fell on his photograph cube, one of those clear six-sided cubes which can hold pictures in each side. It contained six different pictures of himself and his wife, Elizabeth. Gregory Cowan had one of those cognitive "Eureka!" leaps when it occurred to him that these represented the same subject from six different approaches, producing six unique products. In fact, the subjects actually looked different from different angles.

Out of that insight, he produced the cubing heuristic, articulated as follows in *Writing: Brief Edition* (1983,11) published by Elizabeth Cowan alone after Gregory's death.

CUBING

Cubing is a technique for swiftly considering a subject from 6 points of view. The emphasis is on swiftly and 6. Often writers can't get going on a subject because they are locked in on a single way of looking at the topic-and that's where cubing works very well. Cubing lets you have a single point of view for only 3 to 5 minutes, then moves you on to the next point of view. When you've finished cubing, you've spent 18 to 30 minutes, and you've really loosened up the soil of your mind. This technique moves very swiftly and is quite structured.

1. Use all six sides of the cube.

2. Move fast. Don't allow yourself more than 3 to 5 minutes on each side of the cube.

Use All 6 Sides of the Cube: Imagine a cube-think of it as a solid block. Now imagine that each side has something different written on it.

One side of the cube says: Describe it.
Another side says: Compare it.
A third side says: Associate it.
The fourth says: Analyze it.
The fifth says: Apply it.
The sixth side says: Argue for or against it.

For the cubing technique, you need to use all six sides. This is not an exercise in describing, analyzing, or arguing. It is a technique to help you learn to look at a subject from a variety of perspectives. Consequently, doing just one of the sides won't work. Doing just one side is like a mechanical assignment--about "describe this picture." You may decide after doing all six sides that you do want to describe it; but by then your decision will be meaningful and intelligent, based on your having something to say in the form of a description. So remember: cubing takes all six sides.

Expanded Creating Technique:

Move Fast..Don't Allow Yourself More Than 3 to 5 Minutes on Each Side of the Cube. The energy in this creating technique comes from shifting your perspective on the subject often. By moving around the cube, one side after another, in rapid succession, you see that you can look at your subject from a lot of different angles and that you can talk about it in a lot of different ways. You are not hunting for something to say from each perspective; you are taking a quick run into your mind for whatever presents itself on that angle, and the quickness of the run is important. It is the quick switch that makes the Cubing work.

PRACTICING CUBING To practice this creating technique, let's use the imagined picture of a luscious chocolate-covered cherry. Remember the rules: use all 6 sides of the cube and move fast, spending no more than 3 to 5 minutes per side. Look at the chocolate-covered cherry Get your paper and pen ready.

BEGIN: Do each of the 6 steps in order, spending no more than 3 to 5 minutes on each.

1. Describe it. Look at the subject closely and describe what you see. Colors, shapes, sizes, and so forth.

2. Compare it. What is it similar to? What is it different from?

3. Associate it. What does it make you think of? What comes into your mind? It can be similar things, or you can think of different things, different times, places, people. Just let your mind go and see what associations you have for this subject.

4. Analyze it. Tell how it's made. (You don't have to know; you can make it up.)

5. Apply it. Tell what you can do with it, how it can be used.

6. Argue for or against it. Go ahead and take a stand. Use any kind of reasons you want to—rational, silly, or anywhere in between.

When you have finished all six, read over what you have written. If one angle or perspective strikes you as particularly promising, you probably have come up with a focus for an essay. There very likely was one thing you really enjoyed writing during the cubing activity, something that made you smile, something that caused your pen to move faster, something you felt some interest in and even some excitement about. What is amazing and encouraging is that you can find something to say on this frivolous subject, a chocolate-covered cherry! Get used to the pleasure and security of having such a full repertory of creating techniques that you will never be given a subject without knowing at once how to find something you really want to say about it.

STUDENT SAMPLE:

Here is student David Hill cubing the topic "My Home State", which in David's case was Texas. Read his cubings; then see how he used that material in the essay he wrote later.

Texas-big, bold, BIG, GIANT. Everything is big, so big that there's too many different things in it to mention. Texas has girls-girls on the beaches, in the cities, at the parks, in the country. The girls in Texas are something else! The main thing about Texas is that there isn't ONE MAIN THING. DIVERSITY. One can drive all night and never make it out of the state. There are so many different kinds of land-if you get tired of the desert, go to the mountains-if you get tired of the mountains-go to the beach. If you get tired of Texas get the H . . . OUT of here. Economically, it's great.

Texas is similar to and different from itself. Strange -instead of comparing the whole Texas to another whole anything you have to compare a little part of Texas to a whole something else. The beaches-let's compare the beaches- well, now which part? Aren't they all the same? No. Well, now, the South Padre beaches are white-not quite as beautiful as the Bahamas but you can't drink Lone Star on the Bahama beaches. The mountains are another thing.

SOME ARE BIG-like the ones in the dramatic exploration movies. The rivers are like the ones in wilderness movies- movies-maybe that's why the movies are moving headquarters to Texas.

THE SUN-THE HOT, BIG, LONGTIME-RUNNING SUN. Cowboy hats-to keep the sun from burning. The sun of west Texas can make a person crazy if under it for a while-you can't make sandwiches out doors because the sun will toast the bread. Colors-bright colors-paisley colors-psychedelic SUN -old cowboys with leather necks and lines around their eyes from squinting while out in the sun. The weather-where else can it rain for one short 20 minutes and shine brightly soon after, then the next day it'll be cold and the day after hot again, with of course some rain and always THE SUN.

90,000,000 miles of sun, a million beautiful girls, natural flavor, natural psychedelic colors, no preservatives, nothing artificial added. Take above ingredients and mix in one large area-put a little jalapeno pepper in if Mexican flavor is your gig. The only thing left out are the cows-leave them out: they are messy. The Food and Drug administration said that Texas is good for indigestion. Texas is made of a little bit of everything.

You could use it as a wall decoration but you would have to have a BIG WALL!

THE CUBING HEURISTIC

DESCRIBE IT
COMPARE IT
ASSOCIATE IT
ANALYZE IT
APPLY IT
ARGUE FOR OR AGAINST IT

Here is an assignment which employs the cube in its processes:

BIOLOGY 100
Dr. James Scott, Inst.

Today we will be performing microscopic examination of a common substance, blood. Follow the routine you have learned for setting up your equipment and then come to the lab desk to collect a slide containing a sample. After you have looked at your slide through the microscope, record the following structured free write in your lab book. Your instructor will keep time for you while you write a series of six three-minute focused free writes about what you see under your microscope. These free writes constitute a "cubing" exercise on the subject. Following is a list of the ways you will write/think about your   subject:

Describe it.
Compare it.
Analyze it.
Associate it.
Apply it.
Argue for/against it.

When your series is finished, trade it with your lab partner and read hers. Each of you choose from each other's work the particular free write you think is best as a piece of writing about this biological subject. Return the series to your partner. Compare your choices and see if you agree.

For next meeting, expand the chosen free write or another you chose for yourself. Expand it into a two page word-processed paper in which you employ the terminology connected with blood which we have learned today. You may be serious or you may be facetious in this paper, but demonstrate your understanding of what we have learned about the subject of blood as well as your consideration of your own observations during this lab session.

These papers will be evaluated as follows:

An "A" paper will:

1. Demonstrate command of the proper biological terminology, correctly spelled.

2. Demonstrate thoughtful, methodical observation.

3. Display overt organization deriving from a thesis.

4. Contain few errors of usage or mechanics.

A "B" paper will:

1. Demonstrate command of the proper biological terminology, correctly spelled.

2. Demonstrate thoughtful, methodical observation.

3. Display weaker organization or more errors of usage or mechanics.

A "C" paper will:

1. Demonstrate command of the proper biological terminology, correctly spelled.

2. Demonstrate less careful observation.

3. Display weak organization or many errors of usage or mechanics.

Cubing is an effective, though largely neglected, heuristic. Many writers feel that it is too structured or too complicated, but it is an unparalleled way of "pushing the brain" to see what might not have been apparent. It works almost invariably to reveal an approach immediately productive for the thinker/writer/learner. In workshops, I use a provocative photograph as a subject for cubing, usually a photograph of a shirtless male holding a tiny, naked baby. Cubing around such a piece of loaded data is highly revealing for participants.

I am suggesting here that Cowan's heuristic roughly reflects those same rhetorical heuristics discussed in the preceding sections. In fact, I would suggest that an alteration of the cube's sides to directly reflect those six rhetorical heuristics might provide a powerful tool for the thinker/writer/learner who is directly involved in a specific academic subject. If one made definition, process, comparison/contrast, causal analysis, analogy, and classification the sides of the cube, both teacher and students could profit from its use for specific subject matter. The teacher could use this version of cubing to find the best approach for structuring assignments as well as for presentation of material. The student could use it to find a productive learning approach to specific subject matter. Besides inventorying what the student knows about the specific matter, it could provide a mind set for him or her to assimilate difficult concepts.

Look at this same Biology 100 assignment with the altered cube:

BIOLOGY 100
Dr. James Scott, Inst.

Today we will be performing microscopic examination of a common substance, blood. Follow the routine you have learned for setting up your equipment and then come to the lab desk to collect a slide containing a sample. After you have looked at your slide through the microscope, record the following structured free write in your lab book. Your instructor will keep time for you while you write a series of six three-minute focused free writes about what you see under your microscope. These free writes constitute a "cubing" exercise on the subject. Following is a list of the ways you will write/think about your subject:

> Define it.
> Compare/contrast it.
> Analogize it.
> Write about causes or effects associated with it.
> Write about processes associated with it.
> Classify its components.

When your series is finished, trade it with your lab partner and read hers. Each of you choose from each other's work the particular free write you think is best as a piece of writing about this biological subject. Return the series to your partner. Compare your choices and see if you agree.

For next meeting, expand the chosen free write or another you chose for yourself. Expand it into a two page word-processed paper in which you employ the terminology connected with blood which we have learned today. You may be serious or you may be facetious in this paper, but demonstrate your understanding of what we have learned about the subject of blood as well as your consideration of your own observations during this lab session.

These papers will be evaluated as follows:

An "A" paper will:

1. Demonstrate command of the proper biological terminology, correctly spelled.

2. Demonstrate thoughtful, methodical observation.

3. Display overt organization deriving from a thesis.

4. Contain few errors of usage or mechanics.

A "B" paper will:

1. Demonstrate command of the proper biological terminology, correctly spelled.

2. Demonstrate thoughtful, methodical observation.

3. Display weaker organization or more errors of usage or mechanics.

A "C" paper will:

1. Demonstrate command of the proper biological terminology, correctly spelled.

2. Demonstrate less careful observation.

3. Display weak organization or many errors of usage or mechanics.

The altered cube provides ways to think about blood which reflect the structural tools of the academic community. It may give specific students a more efficient way to understand the materials connected with the subject of blood since it provides a framework for specific understanding.

CHAPTER V

STUDENT RESEARCH

Undergraduate research is an area of the academic scene fraught with confusion for both the student and the professor. We seem to have a number of names for undergraduate research projects by which we seem to mean a number of different things. In the workshops on my campus, the subject of undergraduate research projects invariably becomes an issue for extensive discussion. They are commonly assigned as part of course work, and they are commonly regarded by the professors who make the assignments as objects of dread for reading them is regarded as drudgery and angst.

It is usually profitable to begin discussion of the subject with the definition heuristic. Always it is revealing to discover the variation in definitions held by fifteen or so professors from various disciplines as to what exactly a research project assigned to undergraduates consists of. Exploring what skills an undergraduate who attempts an individual's assignments needs is just as revealing. Generally, many of the professors involved find that what they want as a research project is on the order of an annotated literature review of the "chestnuts" in their fields. They are interested in introducing their students to the library's collection of these, having students summarize them to demonstrate both reading and understanding, and having students state some conclusion about this reading and understanding. Few want any independent articulation of thesis or, for that matter, any independent research process. (I have encountered one social scientist whose undergraduate research project involved sending his students to shopping malls armed with questionnaires of their own invention concerning individually articulated topics of their own interest. These students then wrote research reports aimed at outside audiences based on their collected evidence. He was unique.)

In 1993, Carl G. Backman of the Buffalo State College Social Science Department generated the following terms list as a collection of possible definitions:

Alternative terms for types of formal expository papers
Carl Backman. 6/16/93
Research paper (not a term recommended for use):
a paper requiring direct manipulation of the primary raw materials of the discipline. Note that this definition could include lab reports in the laboratory sciences.

Intertextual integration paper: a paper requiring integrated consideration of the messages of more than one printed document.

Literature review: a paper requiring integrated description and evaluation of scholarly works pertinent to a particular topic.

Library research paper: often understood as a literature review, but also often understood as referring to analysis of secondary data (that is, data collected by someone else) rather than description and evaluation of the conclusions/arguments of others.

Annotated bibliography: a collection of summaries (descriptive and possibly evaluative) of the contents of individual texts.

Critique: a paper requiring the writer to reflect evaluatively (and possibly descriptively) upon some stimulus (e.g., an event, an assertion, or even a document or collection of documents).

Reflection: a paper requiring the writer to reflect in unspecified ways to some stimulus.

Essay: a paper presenting and defending one or more points of view on some topic.

I would like Freshman Composition to take as one of its primary foci the intertextual integration paper. The literature review might be considered a species of intertextual integration (a very important species indeed), but differs in subtle yet important ways from a paper that uses other works as an explicit springboard for going beyond the works reviewed.

Leaving Dr. Backman's note at the end of this list was purposeful, for it constitutes evidence of the expected connection between freshman composition and the paths of discourse for the academic community. It seems obvious that the freshman composition program must attend to that connection, keeping apprized of the obligation inherent in teaching freshman composition to prepare students for the expectations of the academic community.

Whatever the definition for undergraduate research that an individual teacher adopts as his or her own, intensive thinking about research project assignments is profitable. Apropos assignment construction as a general consideration, it is most important that teachers invest time in it. Carefully constructed assignments can do much to insure excellent products. Careful consideration of what the projected product of assignments ought to be is as important as any other part of the construction process.

Consider these observations. When a working academic starts a research project, that project is usually involved with some aspect of his or her professional existence which has caused the person to be disturbed in some way. Whether it is something that keeps occurring which cannot be easily understood, or whether it is an insight which comes and then demands to be proven or followed up–whatever the nature of the disturbance, the working academic gets involved enough that he or she feels the need for some sort of inquiry into the matter. There may be a working hypothesis to begin with or part of the research work may be the laying out of a research question. The whole thing proceeds in fits and starts, with many derailments, accidental breakthroughs, wrong paths, restructurings, blank walls. We are all aware of the nature of our own research. The question that comes to mind so often in work with writing-across-the-curriculum is why so many working academics completely disconnect perception of their own research from perception of their students' research. Do we not want our students to be doing the same sorts of things we do, albeit on a lower level? Is it that we are beings so superior to our students that what we do as academics has no resemblance to what we want them to do?

It is fair to say that working academics do research into things in which they are interested. Sometimes they do this research in the interest of their career security; sometimes they do it out of fascination. It is also fair to say, though, that they have a stake in the research, that their research connects with the field in which they have already gained some expertise, and that they proceed out of the training to which they have already given much of their lives. They garner physical or financial support from some part of academe. (The present version of this book was written during a semester's leave provided by The Dr. Nuala McGann Drescher Affirmative Action Leave Program of the New York State United University Professions; it might never have gotten done had that leave not been provided.) They talk about their research to their colleagues, often collaborating on projects. And they have every expectation that their research will take a long time, often years and years, because of all the considerations involved.

How, then, do we think about undergraduate research so as to provide for some of the same considerations? If we cannot, how then can we be so bold as to loosely use the nomenclature "research project"?

In thinking about this, perhaps we first ought to consider that the usual undergraduate research project is expected to take part of a semester so it needs to be limited to some considered boundaries. We do need to think about the nature of our obligations to students with regard to the matter, and make some considered decisions about them. Exactly what are our objectives for assigning undergraduate research projects? If we assign them only because we think our colleagues expect us to do so or because we feel that our students ought to suffer as we did in undergraduate school, then perhaps we just should refrain. We need to have reasons for assigning undergraduate research that are integral to our course objectives as well as to program goals as well as to specific course objectives.

If we only want our students to make the library resources of our field a user-friendly place for themselves, then let us affirm that as an objective and structure assignments which make that clear, which will get at that goal. If we want to foster what Dr. Backman calls integrated intertextuality, then let us structure assignments which involve limited references and let us intentionally model that integrated intextuality. If we are interested in fostering and training our undergraduates as independent researchers, then let us guide them to their own research questions in ways that resemble our paths to our own research questions.

Perhaps the underlying thesis for all research projects of whatever kind is this: "Here is a report about what happened to me as I made an inquiry. First let me tell you what I knew and suspected to begin with. Then let me tell you what I found out as I investigated what other people had to say about the subject and/or as I investigated it for myself. Let me end with what I know now as a result of my investigation." "I" am involved in it from start to finish; if "I" am not involved, then the product *will* be angst for anybody to read.

THE "I-SEARCH" ASSIGNMENT

Ken Macrorie in *The I-Search* (1992) which is the later version of a book originally called *Telling Writing* (1978?), has examined extensively the issue of research. Macrorie contends that nobody should be forced either to do meaningless research projects or to read meaningless research projects. He is sure that the only justifiable investment of time in research for anyone is investment in a subject about which the researcher *needs to know*. His advice, then, is for us to give time to helping our students articulate a research question, that is what it is that they need to know in our disciplines. He advises a lot of heuristic writing for students to be able to accomplish that goal. He advises us to spend our energies in contriving ways to get students to need to know. Macrorie certainly has revolutionized the way we look at student research, but his stance asks us to yield decision making power to students and to foster student voice in a way which will materially affect pedagogy. The Macrorie "I-Search" probably comes the closest to providing students with the opportunity to do and write about research resembling that done and written about by working academics.

Somewhere between the research assignment list aimed at getting students to go to the library to read some articles and Macrorie's "I-Search" is the place that most professors end up after they have examined their practices and pedagogy relative to the matter of undergraduate research. The implemented results of such consideration, though, will almost certainly result in the amelioration of angst for both students and teacher.

Following are examples of research assignments made by teachers who have done some of this examination. Notice the degree to which generative heuristic writing is employed in the initial stages of the assigned work. Notice, too, that most of them insure that the teacher will not be reading cold papers because they involve discourse between teacher and student throughout. The teacher comes to the final product familiar with its territory, assured that he or she will not be reading a paper written by someone's mother, and able to make faster, better judgements in the light of prior experience with the project.

Following are examples of some research assignments which integrate generative and structural heuristics. Note that the assignments contain their grading criteria.

SOC100 Introduction to Sociology
Professor Carl Backman,
Department of Social Science,
Buffalo State College

Formal Writing Assignments on the Micro-Macro Connection

OVERVIEW

The purpose of this series of assignments is to help you find something sociological to say about the micro-macro connection. You will do so first by identifying different forms of discussion of this connection in works I will identify for you. Then you will write a paper containing your own sociological thinking on the topic.

DETAILS

These assignments will involve four written papers, three of them review papers and one a reflection paper.

Review papers. Each review paper will have the same format. I will give you two or three readings to review. For each reading you will choose three dimensions from the Cowan cube and tell me how they are reflected in the writing. That is, assume that the author(s) used the cube in preparing their work, and describe how the results of their cubing work is reflected in their paper. Recall that the six dimensions of the cube are 1) describe it, 2) compare it, 3) associate it, 4) analyze it, 5) apply it, and 6) argue for or against it. You can use different dimensions for each paper you review. At this point you are simply identifying these dimensions in the work of someone else, so you are not expected to attempt to integrate them or even suggest how the author(s) do so.

Structurally, your paper should have a separate section for each reading. Clearly delineated within each section should be a subsection for a brief synopsis of the reading, a subsection for the first dimension you have used, a subsection for the second, and a subsection for the third.

These papers must be typed (or printed) with the usual standards (one inch margins, double-spaced, a bibliography, and standard English spelling, grammar, and punctuation). Two copies must be submitted, one for me, one for your review group.

Reflection papers. By the time the reflection paper is due you will have discovered that sociologists believe there is substantial interplay between individual level social behavior and the behavior of larger social structures. Here I want you to write an essay on the interconnectedness of the micro and macro levels of social life. Describe two important ways in which your personal behavior and the personal behavior of other college students of your age is affected by larger social structures.

Also describe two ways in which your personal behavior and the behavior of other individuals like you affects larger social structures. Convince me that the connections are as you say they are and that they are important. If, as is likely, it is appropriate to refer to other sources (e.g., the assigned reading for this course or other reading you have done to prepare for this paper), be sure to do so. Assume your audience is intelligent college students who may not have taken any sociology.

EVALUATION

For both types of papers, plagiarism (defined for my purposes as copying 5 or more words in a row from someone else's work without either quotation marks or a block quote) will result in a failing grade for the paper. If allowed by the College's judicial code, plagiarism may lead to further punishment for academic misconduct.

Review papers. The most important element in the review papers is your ability to identify primary points made by the authors in their discussions of the micro-macro dimension. Also important, but of lesser importance, is appropriate use of the cube. (I have you use the cube not so much because it is itself important as because I want you to understand some useful ways of thinking about and writing about a phenomenon. One way to develop such an understanding is to see it in action in the works of more practiced thinkers and writers.) For purposes of evaluation, I will individually evaluate each dimension for each of the papers you have reviewed. Within each dimension I will award 1) up to five points for the congruence between what you claimed the author said and what I feel the author said, [*this part of the assignment does not reflect the sentiments of this author.*]

2.) up to four points for how important the ideas you have identified are relative to those you could have used within the dimension, and 3) up to three points for how appropriately you are using the dimension of the cube you claim to be using. Papers that are not typed or computer printed, that are not double spaced, or that do not have approximately one inch margins all around will lose two letter grades; otherwise I will not grade on the basis of writing mechanics except insofar as the mechanics interfere with your ability to make clear what you mean in your writing. However, your colleagues will review your paper for compositional strengths and weaknesses.

Reflection paper. Reflection papers will receive two grades, one for content and one for composition.

Content. About each of the four examples you present, I will ask five questions: 1) Does the specified micro-macro connection actually reflect the micro-macro dialectic? 2) How well does the paper support the assertion of a connection? 3) Is the connection important? 4) Is the assertion of importance well supported? 5) Is the level within the macro system clearly identified, that is, is it for instance a group level, subcultural level, or societal level phenomenon? I will weight each of the five questions equally in my overall evaluation of your paper's content.

Composition. I will evaluate your paper as a composition in five areas, each of which will receive equal weight: 1) overall structure and direction, 2) style, 3) sentence structure, 4) word usage, and 5) mechanics. Overall structure and direction. In this area I am interested in your use of structure and guideposts to enhance the clarity of the messages in your paper. Mechanically, this refers to appropriate sectioning of the paper, carving your work into paragraphs appropriately, providing good introductions and summaries, and managing transitions smoothly. Style. This refers to, among other things, the tone, vividness, precision, and liveliness of your writing. It also refers to the ways in which you use the ideas of others and give them credit for their ideas. It often reflects your mode of argumentation. Mechanically it refers to your vocabulary, the use of examples, passive vs. active voice, and sentence variety. It also refers to consistency in word and sentence use. Sentence structure. Are there run-ons or sentence fragments? Are words in appropriate order? Word usage. Are proper verb tenses used, do pronouns and antecedents agree, are words used in ways that are consistent with both their definitions and their connotations? Mechanics. This deals with spelling, punctuation, capitalization, margins, line spacing and formats for bibliographic referencing. The following scheme will be used to evaluate mechanics:

A   No more than: .5 spelling/capitalization errors per page, .5 punctuation or grammatical errors per page, .25 referencing errors per page, .1 margin/line spacing error per page, and 1 bibliography section error per page.

B   No more than 1 error per page of each type.

C   No more than 3 errors per page of each type.

D   No more than 4 errors per page of each type.

D- No more than 6 errors per page of each type.

Pluses and minuses will be based on how egregious the errors are (e.g., sentence fragments are worse in my book than subject-verb number agreement). If I hit a bad spell in your paper that goes on for a couple of pages, I will probably stop marking your errors and give you a mechanics evaluation based on what I've seen up to the point where I give up on your mechanical disaster.

CHAPTER VI

EVALUATING STUDENT WRITING

The best way to begin improving student writing is to banish three popular beliefs that frustrate students and teachers. One is the belief that instructors should write a lot in the margins and between the lines. Another is that instructors ought to know and use a lot of specific grammatical rules and grammatical terms if they want to comment effectively. A third is that the most effective responses to student writing are instructor-written comments on the final copy. All three beliefs are false. (MacAllister 59).

DETERMINING WHEN AND HOW TO GRADE

When you assign students to write papers, and they write them and hand them in, then you need to do something with them. Looking at a stack of papers half a foot high can make even the most dedicated teacher consider a career change. Faculty will not allow themselves to be exhausted by swimming through a sea of student essays. Therefore, we need an evaluation system that is both efficient for faculty and effective for students.

What, after all, is the purpose of evaluation? There are two purposes: one is to assess and reward student performance; the other is to help the student learn. Of those two objectives, the latter seems to be the most important. Yet, often writing assignments are designed and evaluated in such a way that student learning is secondary. Many of our comments on papers seem to be written to justify a grade more than to help the student improve.

ASK YOURSELF THE FOLLOWING ABOUT A RECENTLY GRADED SET OF PAPERS:

1. Are they graded in the "deduct" manner? (You take off points for errors and sometimes the students end up owing you points.)

2. Are there papers in the stack that made you feel uncomfortable–good papers with bad grades or bad papers with good grades?

3. What was your primary emphasis in grading those papers? What were you looking for? Does the grading reflect that emphasis?

4. Is the grade final, or does the student have the option of improving the paper?

5. How have you responded to what the writers are saying?

6. What do you hope your grading will accomplish with these writers?

7. What type of follow-up teaching have you planned after the papers are returned? (Kirby and Liner)

If the questionnaire makes you a little uncomfortable, or if you find yourself spending more time grading a student paper than the student spent writing it, it may be possible to improve your evaluation techniques. The suggestions that follow, gleaned from both research and experience, are intended to shift the emphasis from measuring to learning, and also to ease the burden on faculty who must read and react meaningfully to student writing.

GRADING STRATEGIES

Below are several useful strategies for evaluation, but regardless of the method, keep in mind that if the final paper is to be successful, some earlier writing activity–generative heuristics, proposals, drafts–should be part of the full assignment. Before you even read the strategies below, ask yourself some questions about your current evaluation procedure:

1. What is your primary emphasis in grading? Is the student aware of that?

2. Do you have a "published" grading scale? Does it emphasize surface or mechanical features?

3. Do you respond to ideas as you grade?

4. Do you plan any type of follow-up after the papers are returned so that the assignment becomes a total learning experience?

Performance Grading

This is a relatively simple and clear way to grade. A quantitative method, this technique allows you to establish the performance criteria. If the students meet the criteria, they get the grade. Since this is a strictly quantitative method, you do not include any value judgements about the quality of the work. For example, if you assign a journal in your course, your criterion may simply be a number of pages dealing with specific topics. The disadvantage of this system is obvious: it does not allow the opportunity to recognize superior work.

Holistic Grading

This system is based on the belief that a piece of writing should be regarded as a single unit of expression and evaluated as a whole without being regarded as separate parts as in the analytical system. In order to do this, you would take the stack of papers, quickly reading through without making any marginal comments or notes. As you skim, keeping in mind the assignment objectives and requirements, you will be able to separate the papers into piles corresponding to letter grades based on your impression as to how those have been met. When you have sorted all the papers into evaluative piles, read again to check for consistency within the group.

Analytic Grading

This evaluation breaks down into categories directing the student's attention to specific aspects of the assignment, assigning points to each. The point value is assigned to features identified as important to the writing task at hand.

Time invested in articulating a detailed rubric for grading is time saved when final evaluation of e fully processed writing assignment is done. The best rubrics are those which are negotiated with students, including their input as to what constitutes the criteria for each specific grade.

SOME ASSESSMENT OPTIONS
Compiled by David W. Schwalm

1. Non-Graded Writing
    —costs (gains in writing skill)
    —benefits (better understanding of material, critical thought, improved class discussion)
    —necessary conditions (related to evaluated work, challenging, divergent questions)
    —some examples: one-minute essays, free writes, believing-doubting, see-saw paper, learning log, reading log
2. Holistically Scored Writing
    —costs (gains in writing skill, irrelevance of some criteria)

—benefits (time--20-30 per hour, ease of training)

—how to norm (a. choose criteria; b. grade samples 1-6; reassess criteria; resolve splits; establish scale—use it all)

3.   Analytic Scales

—costs (more time consuming than holistic scoring; limited writing gains, greater difficulty of achieving agreement)

—benefits (more often relevant to particular papers than holistic scoring; still relatively quick-15-20 papers per   hour)

—how to develop (identify significant features and weight them accordingly)

4. Hired Help

—costs (money, validity, instructor awareness of student   problems and progress, gains in writing, student confidence--unless you hire professionals)

—benefits (time, reliability)

—how to do (identify students and funding, train and resolve splits—stay involved)

5. Models Feedback

—costs (transference to individual cases, class time)

—benefits (concreteness of criteria discussions, tune)

—how to do it (holistically score, take hi-mid-lo samples and put on transparency/or xerox, discuss specific features in class)

6. Group Papers

—costs (student protest, coordination and front end design work, hidden weaknesses of individual writers, grading)

—benefits (fewer papers to grade, group work enhanced)

—how to do it (Jigsaw Paper Strategy: assign 4 essays to groups of four students; each student is to read all, write summary of one; give them a question requiring synthesis or

evaluation of the four)

7.   Portfolios and Selective Grading

—costs (limited feedback for students, logistics)

—benefits (fewer papers to grade, revision work)

—how to do it (E.g. assign 5 papers for the term, holistically score all papers each batch, models feedback—written feedback to 20% each time; let them rewrite one paper)

8. The Well Designed Paper: The Principle of Leverage

See Design Checklist on pp.45 For Features)

9. Efficient Written Feedback

—sort holistically into hi-mid-lo

—limit commentary to two or three major points

—note only patterns of error

—focus on substantive vs. formal feedback

UNDERSTANDING THE DOMAINS OF WRITING AND THEIR HIERARCHY

The Virginia Department of Education published a document called the "Domain Scoring Rubric" used in scoring their statewide writing assessment program. The rubric sets forth this useful taxonomy of the domains of writing which provides the professor faced with evaluating student writing a basic language set and understanding of relative importance of the components of academic writing. This taxonomy can be used to undergird whatever evaluation choices a professor may make:
* Composition
* Style
* Sentence formation
* Usage
* Mechanics

An expanded version of the "Domain Scoring Rubric" can be found in Appendix C.

PREPARING ASSIGNMENTS CAREFULLY

The importance of structuring assignments carefully, with clues for the students as to how they should think about the subject matter and reflect that thinking in their writing, cannot be reiterated often enough. You may save a great deal of time in evaluating the students' efforts if you spend some time thinking through your assignments as was discussed earlier in this chapter. You should be aware that assignments and evaluation are parts of a whole.

1. Try to design interesting and thought-provoking assignments that students will enjoy doing and you will enjoy reading. Encourage creativity and risk-taking, but give students clues as to how to proceed.

2. Connect the assignment with your course objectives so that as students complete the writing task they are also learning and interpreting course concepts. Meaningful evaluation should depend largely on how well the students demonstrate mastery of the material and compose it.

3. Assess the demands of the assignment. Do students know how to do what you are asking them to do? We often assume that

students already know how to operate academically, but, in fact, many do not. Providing guidelines, either through a classroom presentation or a handout will let students know exactly what you want and will simplify your evaluation.

Remember that you need to assure yourself that you and your students have the same definitions for terms like compare, analyze, or summarize.

4. Decide in advance what your grading criteria will be. Explain and illustrate those criteria when you give the

assignment with a rubric in which the requirements for each grade letter from "A" through "E" are spelled out. It is quite beneficial to all if the class feels that they have some input into the evaluation rubric. Base the criteria on both the objectives of the course and the demands of the assignment. (More samples of rubrics like Dr. Schwalm's can be found in Appendix C as well as in the sample syllabi in Appendix A.)

EVALUATING THE PAPERS

Effective evaluation should help students improve; it should not just be used to justify a grade. The following suggestions are helpful in dealing with evaluating papers:

I. Always respond initially with something positive. Students need to see that their work has been read and appreciated.

2. Evaluate based on the published rubric without allowing hidden agendas to influence judgment.

3. Make comments that are both descriptive and helpful. Tell students (a)what they are presently doing or (b) what they failed to do and (c) what they need to do to improve in the future.

4. Limit comments, focusing on those items most closely related to the goals of the course.

5. In evaluating, try to respond to an assignment as a whole, looking at what the paper says, how it is organized and how well it meets the needs of the assignment. That is not to say that you should ignore grammar, spelling, punctuation, but when you cite only technical errors, you are not using the assignment as a content-learning device.

6. To streamline the grading process, consider using a check sheet. Such a device, designed to match your assignment, minimizes the need to write lengthy comments. You simply check off areas of strength and weakness in the paper. A check sheet also helps make your grading more consistent by focusing on the criteria you originally established. Some instructors hand out the check sheet when they give the assignment, so that students will know exactly how they will be evaluated. (Sample check sheets can be found in Appendix B.)

7. Conferences with students may also be valuable at the evaluation stage. See the earlier material on conferencing. (adapted from the recommendations of The Two-Year College Development Center)

Three examples of generic rubrics are below. The Domain Scoring Rubric is in Appendix C. general rubric covering writing for a whole semester is contained in Dr. Emile Netzhammer's assignment on pg.183. All of these things illustrate analytical evaluation instruments.

A GENERIC EVALUATION RUBRIC					
General Merit	Low		Middle		High
Ideas	2	4	6	8	10
Organization	2	4	6	8	10
Wording	2	4	6	8	10
Style	2	4	6	8	10
Mechanics					
Usage	1	2	3	4	5
Punctuation	1	2	3	4	5
Spelling	1	2	3	4	5
Manuscript Form	1	2	3	4	5

This second example allows for rapid scoring since checkmarks indicate the presence or absence of the required features. It is possibly most useful as a response to drafts.

		yes	no	
Composing	I.	___	___	Ideas are insightful.
		___	___	Ideas are original.
Organization	II.	___	___	Each paragraph has a controlling idea.
Mechanics	III.	___	___	There are many misspellings.
		___	___	There are serious punctuation problems.

The third example is much more highly articulated:

Analytical Scoring Rubric
By David W. Schwalm

Score of 6: superior
   -Addresses the question fully and explores the issues thoughtfully.
   -Shows substantial depth, fullness, and complexity of thought.
   -Demonstrates clear, focused, unified and coherent organization.
   -Is fully developed and detailed.
   -Evidences superior control of diction, syntactic variety, and transition; may
      have a few minor flaws.

Score of 5: Strong
   -Clearly addresses the question and explores the issues.
   -Shows some depth and complexity of thought.
   -Is effectively organized.
   -Is well developed, with supporting detail.
   -Demonstrates control of diction, syntactic variety, and transition; may have
a few flaws.

Score of 4: Competent
   -Adequately addresses the question and explores the issue.
   -Shows clarity of thought but may lack complexity.
   -Is organized.
   -Is adequately developed, with some detail.
   -Demonstrates competent writing; may have some flaws.

Score of 3: Weak
   -May distort or neglect parts of the question.
   -May be simplistic or stereotyped in thought.
   -May demonstrate problems in organization.
   -May have generalizations without supporting detail or detail which should
      support generalizations may be undeveloped.
   -May show patterns of flaws in language, syntax or mechanics.

Score of 2: Inadequate
   -Will demonstrate serious inadequacy in one or more of the areas specified
      for the 3 paper.

Score of 1: Incomplete
   -Failed attempts to begin discussing the topic.
   -Deliberately off-topic papers
   -Paper so incompletely developed as to suggest or demonstrate
incompetence.
   -Paper wholly incompetent mechanically.

DEALING WITH ERRORS

Many students have the idea that correctness in writing only counts in an English class. They are often capable of writing better papers once they are encouraged to take the trouble. Students have to be made to realize that taking care with their written work is equally important in all their classes. If your intent is to improve students' usage and mechanics in writing, you might consider the following suggestions:

1. Determine your skills and priorities. Try to help students with problems that (a) you understand and (b) you have time to deal with.

2. Establish a limited set of editing conventions that students must observe. Require students to proofread for these features such as acceptable paragraphing, complete sentences, reasonable spelling, or whatever you believe is important to your assignment.

3. Look for patterns in students' errors. Are there some that simply indicate lack of proofreading or are there some that suggest the student is confusing the conventions of spoken and written language? Are there some that can be eliminated by the student's learning a simple rule?

4. Avoid covering the student's paper with comments and corrections. Recent research indicates "that many teachers tax themselves unnecessarily with copious written commentary" (MacAllister 61). Muriel Harris has concluded that "The amount of useful information students derive from a graded paper, above a certain minimal level, is in inverse proportion to the amount of instructor notation on the page" (Harris, 91). Identify a few important areas and limit your comments to these areas.

5. Refuse to accept papers that are carelessly done. Rather, insist that students rewrite the paper, making them responsible for the quality of the paper and not you.

6. If you feel that the student has debilitating usage/mechanics problems, you should not feel that forced to handle those problems alone. Insist that the student seek help from tutorial agencies within the college such as writing centers. In fact, this help could be factored into the assignment grade. When cooperative learning or helping groups are built into course structure, students can act as resources for each other to help with usage/mechanics problems.

INCORPORATING WRITING INTO PEDAGOGY

This book contains many ways in which you can profitably use writing intensive techniques to teach, but none of them can be effective for you unless you make them your own. You need to gain command of heuristic writing, see for yourself its effectiveness. Adaptation or re-invention of itstechniques will follow naturally to fit the requirements of your own discipline, your own students, and your own pedagogy. Only then can you gain the fullest benefit from using writing to teach.

For some readers, the incorporation of writing intensive techniques into their professional lives will mean major change. For others, it may only be an enlargement or enhancement of their current practice. Whichever of those readers you are, the work you do to in incorporating them will benefit you, your students, and your academic community as well as the larger academic community as a whole. In Appendix A, which follows this section, are some more sample assignments and syllabi. These were created by professors on the campus of SUNY College at Buffalo, also known as Buffalo State College. . These are their re-inventions of writing intensive techniques. From them, you may glean suggestions and materials for your own syllabi and assignments. Use their ideas, but remember–you have to re-invent for yourself. Your investment of time and creativity will be profitable! From assignment to evaluation, student writing is a tool for student learning. Both the teacher and the student benefit from the use of ***WRITING TO LEARN; WRITING TO TEACH!***

SYLLABI FOR WRITING
INTENSIVE COURSES

These materials are directly quoted from selected syllabi written by participants in workshops on "Using Writing to Teach" held on the SUNY College at Buffalo campus, also known as Buffalo State college. They are:

I. Dr. Emile Netzhammer–COMM 332W: Contemporary
    Issues in Broadcasting
II. Mr. William Schieder–NFS 105: Food and People:
    Interactions and Issues
III. Dr. R.C.Stein–BIO 405–Organic Evolution
IV. Dr. Michael Littman–OEC 301W: Principles of
    Occupational Education

Each of these excerpts has helpful application examples of the principles explored in this guidebook.

I. COMM 332W   CONTEMPORARY ISSUES IN BROADCASTING
Dr. Emile Netzhammer, Instructor

In his syllabus, Dr. Netzhammer carefully articulates assignments which use writing for conceptual development as well as for products. Particularly notable are his rubrics for evaluating final papers.

...

OBJECTIVES: This course is designed to provide students with substantive knowledge on major issues currently affecting the broadcast industry and to develop critical thinking skills to analyze such issues. This course is also designed to familiarize students with the popular, trade and scholarly literature regarding broadcasting. Finally, this course is designed to expose students to different views and philosophies of broadcasting.

WRITING REQUIREMENTS:

TERM PAPER: Students will be responsible for writing and presenting a 10-page paper analyzing a particular television or radio program. The program must be recorded by the beginning of the fourth week of class. The paper should analyze the program based on the theoretical material discussed throughout the semester, as well as any other theories deemed relevant by the student. Obviously, some class material will be more relevant than other material, depending on the chosen program. The students should also integrate articles discussed in class and additional research into their papers. This research may come from scholarly publications, such as Journal of Broadcasting and Electronic Media or Critical Studies in Mass Communication, trade publications, such as Broadcasting Magazine, Advertising Abe or Columbia Journalism Review, or the popular press. During the last two weeks, the class will view some of the videotapes and discuss the program. A draft of the paper is due November 18. Final papers are due December 9. The term paper is worth 25% of the final grade.

THOUGHT PAPERS: Ten times during the semester students must complete a three-page, typewritten thought paper. These papers usually will be collected on Mondays. Unless a specific topic is given, any focused topic pertaining to the media and society is acceptable. Each paper should respond to the issues raised in class and the readings. It should also integrate examples of radio and television programming relevant to the issues discussed in class. Each paper must be typed and collected in a three-prong folder. Each paper is worth 2 points. (Students submitting less than five thought papers will receive an "E" for the class.)

JOURNALS: Students should keep a notebook that contains the class writing exercises and any random thoughts about the media or the class. The class exercises are primarily brief writing tasks designed to encourage deeper thinking about the topics. The journals will also provide the instructor with feedback on where problems are surfacing. The specific exercises will not be graded, but the journal is worth 5%.

JOURNAL ASSIGNMENTS

In Contemporary Issues in Broadcasting, we will use a number of writing exercises as a preparation for class discussion. The exercises are designed to help students focus on a particular topic and to help students think more deeply about the topic of discussion on a particular day. They are also designed to give you ideas for thought papers and your term paper. These exercises should be completed in a marble notebook. You can also include any random thoughts about topics related to the class in your notebook. The journals will be collected periodically, but they will not be graded. The following are some examples of the types of things we will be doing in class.

Focused Free writing Exercises

Generally, class time in COM 332 is spent discussing a particular topic related to the media and society. This always involves a set of readings and usually involves a text (a television program) viewed in class. Focused free writing is an exercise for organizing your thoughts before discussion. Focused free writing has three rules:

    1) You must write for a set period of time;

    2) Your pen must not stop moving during that time;

    3) You may not stop to make corrections.

Much of what you write will be trash. Even more will be uninspired. Your task is to find the insight among the trash. We will use a number of variations of this exercise.

Composition Exercises

Since the course involves the use of specific terms related to the profession, you may be asked to write a brief composition utilizing those words. This will help us to ensure that everyone is giving similar meaning to the terms used.

Random Thoughts

From time to time, everyone has an inspired thought about a topic that they don't know what to do with. Anytime you have an interesting thought about mass communication and society, write it in your journal. This will help you to become more aware of the pervasive influence of media in society. No thought is too brief or too stupid to qualify for inclusion in your notebook. When it comes time to select topics for papers, you'll be very glad you did.

THOUGHT PAPERS

Ten times during the semester students must complete a three page, typewritten thought paper. These papers usually will be collected on Mondays. Unless a specific topic is given, any focused topic pertaining to the media and society is acceptable. Each paper should respond to the issues raised in class and the readings. It should also integrate examples of radio and television programming relevant to the issues discussed in class. Each paper must be typed and collected in a three-prong folder. Each paper is worth 2 points. (Students submitting less than five thought papers will receive an "E" for the class.) Assignments for the first and second thought papers are explained below. Generally, however, students will select their own topics for the thought papers. The thought papers are designed to advance critical thinking about the media by getting you to write in depth on a single topic. They do not have to be polished final drafts. Don't spend all your time on grammar, spelling and punctuation. They count, but the major focus of my evaluation will be your ideas. All thought papers must meet the following criteria:

1. They must have one clear assertion that can be discussed for 2.5 to 3 pages. Don't try to discuss several unrelated ideas in one paper.

2. The assertion must be related to the very broad issue of mass communication and society. In other words, relate it to the class.

3. They must be typed, double spaced. Your paper can be edited in pen. It doesn't have to be perfect.

The thought papers will be assigned a CHECK—PLUS, CHECK or CHECK—MINUS based on the following criteria:

CHECK-PLUS

content: The paper is insightful. The paper addresses the specific topic if one has been assigned. It has one central assertion and support for that assertion. It meets the criteria outlined above.

organization: The central assertion is clear. Examples develop the assertion. The paper has a cohesive, logical order. mechanics: Mechanical errors aren't intrusive.

NOTE : To receive a CHECK-PLUS, the paper does not have to be error free. It does not have to reflect the views of the instructor. It does not have to be polished.

CHECK

content: The paper goes beyond class discussion. The paper addresses the specific topic if one has been assigned. It has one central assertion and support for that assertion. It meets the criteria outlined above.

organization: The central assertion is discernable. The paper includes support for the assertion. mechanics: Mechanical errors don't obscure basic meaning.

NOTE: To receive a CHECK, the paper does not have to provide new insight.

CHECK-MINUS

content: The paper repeats class discussion. The paper addresses a topic unrelated to class. It does not meet the criteria outlined above.

organization: The central assertion is not discernable. The paper is underdeveloped (no support for assertion). The paper is unclear. mechanics: Mechanical errors obscure basic meaning. NOTE: A CHECK-MINUS is equivalent to not turning in a paper.

First Thought Paper:

As we will discuss in class, an individual's understanding of a program is influenced by the beliefs and values each of us holds. A mediated message will have different meaning for different people. For example, someone who is very liberal will take something different from Firing Line than someone who is conservative. An African-American Lesbian will interpret The Cosby Show differently than a white, heterosexual man. In your first thought paper, you are to look deep within yourself to identify those aspects of your culture that influence the way you understand a television program. Give examples of programs you like or dislike, and explain what elements of your identity affect your enjoyment and understanding of a program. Don't rely on obvious answers.

Second Thought Paper:

Television programs, even those designed exclusively for entertainment, promote very specific beliefs, values and ideologies. The Waltons and Little House on the Prairie, for example, arguably promoted traditional family values. Recognizing the manner in which these beliefs are encouraged and promoted in television programming is an important step in understanding the role of the media in society.

This assignment is designed to help you begin to recognize the system of beliefs promoted through television:

Watch a 30-minute situation comedy. In your second thought paper, address the following:

1. Briefly describe the episode. (one short paragraph)

2. Select a belief, value or ideology that is consistently promoted during the episode.

3. Give three examples from the program in which that belief is promoted, and discuss how you think each example promotes the belief.

II. NFS 105: FOOD AND PEOPLE: INTERACTIONS AND ISSUES
Mr. William Scheider, Inst.

Mr. Scheider has some notable assisted writing invitations in this syllabus. Also his rubric for evaluating papers is valuable.

...

The amount of material in this course is large and diverse, and class sessions can only provide basic concepts relating to each topic. Writing papers is a way to stimulate students to explore certain topics to a greater depth in directions that are interesting and relevant to them.

Assignment #1: The material we have covered in class provides a framework for studying the diets of other cultures and ethnic groups. We have already examined basic dietary characteristics of some of the major ethnic groups in the U.S. This paper provides an opportunity to explore a specific ethnic eating pattern in greater depth. Pick an ethnic group and write a paper about its traditional eating patterns according to the following criteria:

a. Selecting an ethnic group- you may want to choose a group in your own ethnic background, such as Northern Italian, Jewish, African-American, Mexican-American, and so on. You may choose a form of vegetarianism or the modern American diet instead of an ethnic group.

b. What to find out about- research the ethnic group's traditional eating patterns, including, but not limiting yourself, to the following:

1) Staple sources of energy, such as corn, rice, cassava, and beans.

2) Major protein sources, including complementary relationships.

3) Important fruits and vegetables.

4) Important beverages.

5) Unique methods for preparing (including spices), serving, and eating food.

6) Why these particular foods and methods are used by this ethnic group (i.e. how did they evolve, what functions do they perform).

This focused free-write is intended to show the diversity of reasons people eat. Hopefully, the discussion will generate a list of roles food plays, which can be organized by category (physical, psychological, and sociocultural) and used to illustrate theoretical principles that are covered in lecture.

Assignment #2: At the beginning of a unit about food hazards (e.g. additives, pesticides, and microorganisms), students will be asked to do the following:

"We are constantly bombarded with information about what is hazardous in our food. Some people become anxiety-ridden about what they eat; others cast caution to the wind, figuring they have no control over their risk anyway. I would like you to write about your fears relating to the food you eat and what steps you take to reduce dietary hazards. If you do not have concerns about the safety of your food, discuss why. When I tell you to begin, write continuously for 3 minutes, recording whatever comes into your mind about the topic. When we have finished, I will ask for volunteers to share what they have written."

This exercise is the first step in helping people develop a sound dietary risk management strategy. It will be used as the basis for a discussion aimed at identifying the students' most important food safety concerns. Theoretical concepts about how scientists assess risk can then be combined with the students' personal techniques for reducing risk to develop a practical plan for minimizing hazards without engaging in bizarre, expensive, or unhealthy dietary practices.

Assignment #3: At the beginning of a unit about domestic and world hunger, which will in part examine social, economic, and political causes of the problem, students will be asked to do the following:

"Americans tend to take the abundance and variety of our food supply for granted, and we seldom think about what is involved in bringing it to us. In fact, our food choices have profound social and political consequences for other people in the U.S. and in foreign countries. I would like you to write about eating as a political act. When I tell you to begin, write continuously for 3 minutes, recording whatever comes into your mind about the topic. When we have finished, I will ask for volunteers to share what they have written."

This free-write will be the basis for a discussion intended to broaden students' perspectives about their relationship with the world as a whole. We will generate a "cluster map" with the American diet at the center. Immediate and apparent socioeconomic and political effects will be positioned near the center, and ramifications of these effects will be at successive corners.

III. BIO 405: ORGANIC EVOLUTION
Dr. R. C. Stein, Inst.

Dr. Stein's syllabus contains an example of a cover sheet incorporating evaluation, of a Virginia Department of Education rubric adaptation, and of a full evaluation sheet for the instructor.

...

CLASS POLICIES
PORTFOLIO:
Twelve unannounced short writing assignments will be given during class time, and on the forms provided. The topic will relate to the material assigned for the previous two classes, and take the form of directed writing, such as a short essay question. Each student will submit a portfolio containing ten of these for review before the Thanksgiving recess. Two of the assignments, the student's choice, will be graded for relevance, content and organization. They will not graded for grammar or spelling unless these mechanical aspects detract from other aspects.

WRITTEN REPORT:
The written report will be due on December 2. See the attached sheet for suggestions and regulations. 25 points will be deducted for each calendar day that the first draft and final paper are late.

I) One report is required, and will be expected to be letter perfect, well organized, and in a style suited for publication.

II) The topic is the role of evolutionary principles in a genus, family, or order of organisms of your choice; or the exposition of a particular evolutionary process. This needs to be established with the professor, in consultation, by the end of September.

a) 30 September—Last day for establishing the individual's topic. Please think out your interests in preparation for your consultation with the professor.

b) 16 October class meeting—a proposed bibliography and general discussion to be submitted. At least six literature references shall be cited in the paper, not including the textbook or encyclopedias. At least two of these shall describe original research (primary source) by an individual author. The object of the exercise is to acquaint you with the literature, and locating sources. Adjustment of topic may be necessary, depending upon available material.

c) 4 November class meeting—a rough draft submitted. While this does not need to be "letter perfect", the student should strive to hand in a draft which requires a minimum of editing and rewriting. A 25 point penalty will be subtracted for each calendar day it is late. 1) The draft report shall be at least 3000 words long, It shall be either a computer printout or typed, 12 pt., double-spaced. Leave a wide (1") margin on the right and left of the text for editorial comments and markings. 2) A separate cover page shall be included. 3) A draft of the abstract shall be included on a separate sheet.

d) 2 December class meeting—The final report is due. A 25 point penalty will be subtracted for each calendar day it is late. The report shall include the following:

1) A title page—a model is provided. 2) Signatures of two persons in the class who have read and criticized your paper. 3) A 200-250 word abstract shall be included on a separate sheet. 4) A suitable bibliography. Follow-up on 16 Oct. assignment. 5)The final report will be graded content and organization. The mechanics include spelling, grammar, punctuation, paragraph structure; and clarity, redundancy, relevance, and development of ideas (not necessarily equally or in that order of priority). An information sheet is provided for your guidance. The Style Manual for Biological Journals or Your textbook bibliography shall be followed for literature citations and other mechanics of writing and style.

III) The total number of possible points (300) is equivalent in weight to the final examination. It accounts for almost one-third of the final grade.

WRITTEN REPORT COVER SHEET
TITLE
Author
Date of Submission
Group reader: 1)

GRADE: Biblio. Due 16 Oct.—50 points
     Draft Due 4 Nov.—100 points
     Late Penalty: 25 points per calendar day
Contents:

Presentation:

Mechanics:

Final Report: Due 2 Dec.—150 points Late Penalty: 25 points per calendar
day FINAL GRADE: Maximum 300 points

WRITTEN REPORTS: EVALUATION CONSIDERATIONS
COMPOSITION:
This is the overall structure, focus and elaboration of the topic.
A. Central Idea—What is it? Is it clear?
Present this in your introduction
B. Elaboration—are suitable examples used to support the details
C. Unity and Organization—Does the presentation have a logical flow?
D. Conclusions
Include relevance to situation at hand
STYLE:
This is an expression of the author's view and approach to the problem.
A. Suitable vocabulary
B. Appropriate information
C. Suitable tone—clearly indicating to whom the paper is addressed.
D. Sentence variety
SENTENCE FORMATION:
The use of sentences appropriate to the author and audience.
A. Complete sentences
Avoid run-on sentences
Expansion of coordinate ideas
Hierarchy of ideas through subordination
B. Standard word order
USAGE:
Word-level features related to standard discourse. Grammatically correct.
A. Correct and clear word meanings
Ambiguity
B. Agreement between sentence parts
MECHANICS:

These are the aspects one should check in order to produce a "perfect" paper for submission.

A. Paragraph Format

B. Capitalization

C. Spelling—Use the spell checker on your computer!

D. Punctuation—be especially careful of commas and semicolons.

IV OEC 301W: PRINCIPLES OF OCCUPATIONAL EDUCATION
Dr. Michael Littman, Inst.

Dr. Littman's use of writing groups to facilitate his plans is quite notable. He also adapts the Virginia Department of Education's scoring rubric.

...

COURSE DESCRIPTION: This course is the first course in a sequentially designed teacher education program in occupational education. The student will study the components of the organization and operation of secondary occupational education programs. This course will focus on four major areas. The first is an overview of the history, philosophy, and principles of vocational (occupational) education. The second area includes the educational tools necessary to be a successful teacher such as curriculum, instruction, evaluation, and educational psychology. The third area includes understanding the concerns and feelings of teenagers. The final area includes the academic proficiency to mesh academic skills into the occupational curriculum. The emphasis will be on developing a knowledge base and personal skills necessary for future professional preparations.

COURSE OBJECTIVES: This course is designed to develop competent, effective, and caring teachers by strengthening individual skills and teaching competency. OEC 301W is an organized, logical, and comprehensive treatment of core principles of occupational education. It will afford students the opportunity to assess, monitor, and evaluate their values and commitment to teaching and learning. It will afford the opportunity to visit schools and interact with teachers and students. Most importantly, this course will add essential knowledge that will be useful in other professional preparation courses and in your professional career. An important concern in this course is the ability to DEVELOP ORAL AND WRITTEN COMMUNICATION SKILLS, PROBLEM SOLVING SKILLS, AND TEAM BUILDING SKILLS.

COURSE REQUIREMENTS:

EXAMINATIONS: Three exams will cover assigned readings and class material. Exams will be essay and each exam will be composed of application questions covering course material. Each exam will have a selection of four questions with each student choosing three to answer. One question will be assigned to complete at home.

Assignments– "WHY I WANT TO TEACH" PAPER: a three page typed paper will be developed as part of your teaching portfolio. This paper will be written (draft copy) at the beginning of the semester. Using the instructor's comments and any changes you would want to include, a final paper using the whole writing process must be submitted at the end of the semester. The first paper must be handed in with the second paper to earn credit.

FORMAT: Section I: Major reasons you want to teach. 3 points

Section II: Why teaching is a proper career choice. 4 pts Section III: What can you as a person and you as a teacher do differently for students? 4 pts

Section IV: List your two strongest points and two weakest points now. How will use your strengths in teaching? Briefly describe how you will overcome your weaknesses. 10 pts

PHILOSOPHY PAPER: This 4 page paper using the full writing process should develop your thoughts on and address the following issues:

Format: Section I: The Function of Education

Section II: The Function of General Education

Section III: The Function of YOUR SPECIFIC AREA of OCED

Section IV: How General Education and Your area of OCED can work together in student education.

The student will consult with his/her writing group before submitting the paper to the instructor.

DALE CARNEGIE PAPER: A four page paper using the full writing process that utilizes the key points in two selected chapters of his book.

Format: Section I: Summarize the key points in the chapter.

Section II: Develop a plan to use these points in your everyday life. (i.e., friends, family, others)

Section III: Develop a plan to use these key points in your teaching career and work with students and co-workers. Each chapter should have Sections I-IV.

The student will consult with his/her writing group before submitting the paper to the instructor.

CURRENT EVENT NOTEBOOK: Four articles per month should be selected to write a 2-3 paragraph reaction for each. **Two** articles should relate to **Education**. You should develop two distinct reactions. One from the viewpoint of a parent and one from the viewpoint of an educational professional.

One article should relate to **business** and should explain the important points in the article and develop two concepts you can teach. One article should relate to a **social** concern that impacts on school and/or education. Briefly explain the social concern and whether it would be useful for a class discussion.

JOURNAL ARTICLE: One critique of a professional journal article is required. The purpose of this assignment is to view current occupational education practices and strategies. It should be no more than three pages typewritten. Please enclose a PHOTOCOPY of the article.

Format: Section I: Reason you chose article. (relevance) 5pts Section II: Summary of major(key) points.   8pts

Section III: Importance of article to a future teacher. Section IV: What YOU learned from the article. 10pts

Section V: How this information will be HELPFUL in

your career. 10 pts

SCHOOL OBSERVATION JOURNAL: Written-At each school you visit you should keep a journal of your feelings about the school, classroom, program, instructor, students, and other related factors. ONE OBSERVATION following the attached format must be submitted and presented to class. Oral-Each student will present a six minute presentation on their school observation at the end of the semester.

WRITING: THIS IS A WRITING INTENSIVE COURSE SO PLAN ACCORDINGLY. Each assignment is required to use headings to separate each section. Since writing is a critically important professional and personal skill all assignments are expected to be professionally developed and presented. Please staple assignments and do not use folders. Cover sheets are not needed. Your name should only be placed on the final page at the bottom.

Twenty percent of your grade will be from a written component analysis and eighty percent will be allocated to content. This means all words should be correctly spelled using proper sentence structure. Assignments that are unacceptable will not be graded and must be rewritten. All rewrites will lose 10%. All late assignments will also lose 10%.

YOU WILL RECEIVE THE GRADE YOU EXPECT IF I RECEIVE THE WORK I EXPECT!

HELPFUL HINTS:

"Education in the deepest sense is continuous and lifelong and in essence unfinished. What we think we already know is often less helpful than the desire to learn." James Hilton- English novelist

"An investment in knowledge pays the best dividend." Ben Franklin

"Do your best." Buddha to his followers.

"It is not what is in front of you nor what is behind you but what is inside of you." Emerson.

Be KNOWLEDGE CONSCIOUS, not GRADE CONSCIOUS.

"A mind is a wonderful thing to save." Willa Spivey, Business Dept. secretary.

WRITING

This course will emphasize writing skill development. It is important that we, as future teachers, become role models for proper writing skills and have the ability to further develop and refine our student's writing skills. This course is thus structured so that we can develop, practice, and refine our own writing skills. *Write we must!*

It is critical to remember that writing is developmental and individual. Each of us has our own style and purpose in writing which should be taken into account in a subsequent evaluation.

WRITING GROUPS

The purpose of the writing group is to have students work with their peers to review, to critique, and to provide feedback on certain major writing assignments. The bottom line goal is to improve your writing and to allow you to review other student's written work. This should improve your personal skills and professional competency in writing. Group input should help in the drafting, revision, and editing of papers. The groups will meet during class time and other times at the discretion of group members. Writing Group membership is encouraged but not mandatory.

THE WRITING PROCESS
I. PRE-WRITING
II. DRAFTING
III. REVISION
IV. EDITING/PROOFREADING
V. FINAL VERSION
WRITING HIERARCHY
COMPOSING: Focusing, structuring and elaborating the writer's message.
o Central Idea
o Elaboration
o Unity
o Apparent Organization
o Organization Facilitates Message
STYLE: Shaping and controlling sentences to achieve purpose of message.
o Information Selected
o Vocabulary Selected
o Suitable Tone
o Real Voice
o Sentence Variety
SENTENCE FORMATION: Composition of competent, appropriately mature sentences.
o Standard Word Order
o Complete Sentences
o Avoidance of Run-Ons

o Expansion through Coordination

USAGE: Word-level features related to standard informal discourse.

o Agreement (subject-verb, pronoun-antecedent)

o Correct Word Meanings

o Inflections (verb, noun, pronoun)

o Vague Pronoun References

MECHANICS: Symbols and cues that allow understanding of written text.

o Capitalization

o Paragraphing Format

o Punctuation (internal, end)

o Spelling

From: Virginia Department of Education State Education Project (1986).

EVALUATION OF WRITING

Instruction: Please self-evaluate each assigned major paper on the following criteria:

COMPOSING: Focusing, structuring and elaborating the writer's message.

o Central Idea

o Elaboration

o Unity

o Apparent Organization

o Organization Facilitates Message

RATING: High-Low

54321

Comments:

STYLE: Shaping and controlling sentences to achieve purpose of message.

o Information Selected

o Vocabulary Selected

o Suitable Tone

o Real Voice

o Sentence Variety

RATING: High-Low

54321

Comments:

SENTENCE FORMATION: Composition of competent, appropriately mature sentences.

o Standard Word Order

o Complete Sentences

o Avoidance of Run-Ons

o Expansion through Coordination

RATING: High-Low

54321

Comments:

USAGE: Word-level features related to standard informal discourse.

o Agreement (subject-verb, pronoun-antecedent)
o Correct Word Meanings
o Inflections (verb, noun, pronoun)
o Vague Pronoun References

RATING: High-Low54321

Comments:

MECHANICS: Symbols and cues that allow understanding of written text.

o Capitalization
o Paragraphing Format
o Punctuation (internal, end)
o Spelling

RATING: High-Low54321

Comments:

OTHER COMMENTS ON PROCESS OR PRODUCT:

From: Virginia State Education Department (1986)

SOME EXAMPLES OF WRITING ASSIGNMENTS

Writing-to-Learn Assignments
That Increase Student (Not Teacher) Engagement
Or
"Write More - Grade Less"
Compiled by David W. Schwalm

Criteria for Assessing Writing-to-Learn Assignments:
1. It requires no elaborate explanation.
2. It gets students to reflect on what they've learned and what they don't yet know.
3. It is clearly and immediately related to course material.
4. It is short and can be quickly read by an instructor.
5. It doesn't appear to students to be busy work because it leads somewhere--a better grade on an assignment, better understanding of crucial course material.

GENERIC WRITING INTENSIVE ASSIGNMENTS
1. One-Minute Essay: As a way of monitoring your class' learning and of stimulating better class discussion and closer reading, consider the one-minute essay. It simply asks two questions: 1. What's the most significant thing you

learned? 2. What's the most significant question you're left with? The questions can be asked at the beginning of class about a reading assignment in order to stimulate discussion or at the end of class about the day's discussion in order to monitor student comprehension of course material.

2. Joint Responses: Have students trade papers and read what others wrote in response to a question (e.g. a one-minute essay). Have 2-3 students write a joint response and then read it aloud to the rest of the class. These written responses need not be graded, perhaps just collected and checked off. But let students know their responses are valuable to you.

3. MicroThemes: Longer is not always better. Have students write reviews of magazine articles, books, films, etc. that must fit on a 4x6 note card. This helps them to get rid of excess verbiage and to focus on the pertinent information. Microthemes are always tightly structured, giving students a format that allows them to focus on your content objectives. You might provide a topic sentence in which a controversial claim is made. Give students the choice of agreeing or disagreeing with the claim. Then ask them to offer three reasons with two pieces of evidence for each reason in support of their position on the claim. Or, going the other direction, you might provide students with a list of factual statements about an important subject in your course, and have them write an appropriate topic statement that would sum up the relationship of those statements.

4. Writing Roulette: This tool can be used in conjunction with the one-minute essay or any short response to class material. Ask students to write in response to a question for several minutes. Then have them pass their papers to the person behind them. Their task then is to pick up where the other student's paper left off--commenting, clarifying, and adding to what they read. Stress to the students that they should try to keep the flow from the previous writer going. Repeat this process up to four times (adding time for reading) and return the papers to the original writers. Collect them and read some aloud to the class and respond by clarifying and re-emphasizing important points.

5. Believing-Doubting Game: As an invention strategy for argumentation topics, consider using the believing-doubting game. Believing-doubting is basically a variant on "brainstorming". You begin by writing a controversial statement about your material on the board. Then ask them, either individually or in small groups, to identify every reason they can think of to support that statement. After several minutes, have them stop and then identify every reason they can think of for doubting or rejecting that statement. During each of these two periods, no counter-arguments can be put forth. Now ask students to identify their the three best reasons for doubting and for believing and have them write them on the board. As a class then, identify the strongest reasons on both sides. These then could form the basis of a microtheme or an out-of-class journal assignment.

6. Data Sets: In some courses, data set assignments that ask
students to draw conclusions from charts, graphs, tables or even a series of
factual statements (a la' Harper's Index:) are good ways to get students writing.

7. Descriptive outlining: For short reading assignments, consider the use of
descriptive outlining. A descriptive outline requires students to indicate what
each paragraph says (a paraphrase)and what each one "does" (e.g. supports a
claim, offers examples of a principle, cites a different point of view, etc.) . These
are very intensive sorts of exercises and can be deadly with long pieces of
writing. But for getting students to close-read short, dense passages of writing,
they can work very effectively. You might have students working in groups
divide up a long essay or chapter into shorter pieces and assign a student to do a
descriptive outline of each piece. They could then teach each other their
particular piece.

8. Idea Maps: (A variation of clustering or webbing.) As a substitute for
traditional outlining at the beginning of the writing process, consider using the
idea map. Idea maps organize information visually in order of increasing
particularity without any rigid notions of hierarchy. Have students draw a circle
around their main topic idea. Then draw lines out from the circle with associated
ideas connected by "strings" (short lines). Idea maps allow students to see all
their ideas at once, without having to commit to a formal organizational scheme.
(Formal outlining is a great strategy for helping students move from a rough draft
to a second draft.)

9. The List: Sometimes it is more effective for students to
practice with shorter forms of writing. For example, students can sometimes
accomplish much by making a list. As they write the list, one thought will often
lead to another. They can make lists of:

    steps in a process
    causes
    effects
    reasons
    examples
    items
    suggestions
    ideas
    conclusions

10. Journals: Have students write in a daily or weekly journal structured so
that they are responding to specific questions that you've devised or generic
questions such as those in the one-minute essay (See above #1). Have students
write for 10 or 15 minutes at a time, outside of class or for shorter periods at the
beginning of class if you want to use the journals to promote class discussion.
Good questions to ask include: how to apply a general principle in a given

situation or how to define a "borderline" case. Above all, avoid questions with one right answer. Again, it's important that journal questions focus on the key course concepts; a good journal would comprise an ideal "study guide" for your course final.

11. Reading Journals: Have students respond to outside reading to help make them more critical readers. The one-minute essay works well as a reading guide. If you decide to develop "customized" questions for the reading, avoid informational questions that ask students simply to retrieve isolated bits of information. Summaries are OK, particularly if you have them write multiple summaries of varying length or compare their summaries to those of their peers.

12. Dialectical Notebook: The most open-ended journal recommended is the "dialectical notebook. Half the notebook is used for observation or summary while half is used for reflection on the summary. Such notebooks are particularly useful in classes which require primary research or have an interest in foregrounding methodology or process.

13. Free writing: At the beginning of a lecture, discussion, chapter, unit, or period, ask students to write nonstop for five to ten minutes on what they know about the concept to be introduced. This will focus them on the learning to be taught, and if you call on them to share what they've written, you may be surprised at what they know or don't know about the subject.

14. More Free writing: Use the same type of free writing activity at the end of a lecture, film, chapter, etc. Ask students to write nonstop about what they've learned and how it's connected to previous material in the course. Again, this can be a springboard for discussion as students read or paraphrase their writing aloud. Students can also share their free writings with others.

15. Notebooks: You may want to have students keep these free writings in a notebook, date the entries, and collect them at the end of a quarter. Then just count the entries and award points for completion.

16. Note cards: Try using note cards instead of paper. After a reading, film, lecture, etc., ask students to write down a "wondering" question or a potential test question about concepts presented. Redistribute the cards, asking each student to respond to the question he or she receives. Then ask students to read their questions and responses aloud.

COURSE SPECIFIC WRITING INTENSIVE ASSIGNMENTS

These assignments which follow have been developed by faculty teaching writing-emphasis courses at Buffalo State College. Each was designed to achieve the instructor's course objectives. Some of them direct the student writers to address a specific audience, making the writing situation more realistic and also requiring students to process course material and to put it down in understandable language, thus enhancing their own grasp of the material.

EXAMPLE 1: The first example demonstrates how to develop a piece of writing from the ungraded prewriting stage through graded, polished writing. It demonstrates objectives in giving the assignment. It uses writing as a method of learning, and the writing assignments vary according to what the learning objectives are.

COMMUNICATION 418 - Dr. Marian Deutschman
SITUATION
A local business publication publishes a letter from a business major at a local college who complained about "parasites" in business. She claims these are functions which reduce profits
but do not contribute to the "bottom line". She sees public relations as the worst of these parasites, While noting that advertising has been shown to increase sales, she says nobody seems to be able to measure the effects of public relations. She calls it "a fraud perpetuated by wasted writers who send out thousands of releases that few publish and nobody reads."
ASSIGNMENT
Part I - Prewriting
In preparation for writing a 200-500 word letter to the editor of the business publication , I am requiring a prewriting exercise called "focused free writing". This technique is intended to induce fluency and to assist you to write this letter.
The rules for this exercise are:
1–Write about the value of public relations.
on that sentence and elaborate on its significance again following rules 2, 3, and 4 as presented for Part I.
Part II
Write a 200-500 word letter to the editor of this business publication. Explain, to your skeptical target audience of business 2–Keep your pen moving at all times. Even if you get stuck, keep writing words. In fact, that's when you're likely to create useable "gems".
3–You may cross out words, but don't go back and correct words or sentences because this disrupts the free flow of ideas and the mental process that connects thinking and writing.
4–Limit yourself to five minutes for this prewriting.
Part III
Select one sentence from the text of your prewriting exercise. It should be a sentence that most appropriately addresses the accusation that public relations does not contribute to the "bottom line". Focus majors, just what public relations is. Include a justification for public relations, discussing its necessity, objectives, and value. Take great care, as a last step, that your letter is technically perfect.

Make certain that your word usage, sentence structure, spelling, abbreviation, and capitalization are correct. Make your final copy absolutely neat and clean with no pencil corrections or strike overs. You will be graded on the persuasiveness of your content and on professional presentation.

Hand in Parts I and II as well. Your prewriting will not be graded but will be discussed with you in a private session about approaching writing assignments with creativity, critical thinking, and less anxiety.

EXAMPLE 2:   Some writing requires no revision and is tailored to reinforcing what is learned. It can be tied closely to other course activities.

SCHOOL OBSERVATION JOURNAL

1. Written–At each school you visit, you should make journal entries about your feelings about the school, classroom, program, instructor, students, and other related factors. One observation following this format must be submitted and presented to the class.

2. Oral–Each student will make a six minute presentation on their school observation at the end of the semester.

EXAMPLE 3:   This assignment focuses heavily on the preparation for writing and extends over a period of time. The writing is a final product directly related to a longer learning experience.

COM 389W: RHETORICAL CRITICISM - Dr. Kerry Sanger

RHETORICAL SITUATION PAPER

You will be responsible for choosing a rhetorical message to work with for the entire semester. The rhetorical situation paper is essentially a paper wherein you will describe the situation that surrounded the communication of your message. We will discuss the components of the paper extensively before you begin to write. The paper will be five to seven pages long. This assignment will be worth 15% of the final grade.

EXAMPLE 4: This writing assignment serves to get students to think about important topics related to the course. It reinforces what is learned and promotes class discussion. Ideas are more important than mechanics.

THOUGHT PAPERS:

Ten times during the semester, students must complete a three-page, type-written thought paper. These papers will usually be collected on Mondays. Unless a specific topic is given, any focused topic pertaining to the media and society is acceptable. Each paper should respond to the issues raised in class and the readings.   It should also integrate examples of radio and television programming relevant to the issues discussed in class. Each paper must be typed and collected in a three-pronged folder. Each paper is worth 2 points. (Students submitting less than 5 thought papers will receive an "E" for the class.)

APPENDIX C

FORMS AND CHECKLISTS

This appendix contains a variety of forms and checklists for various uses:

1. A checklist for evaluating compositions.
2. A checklist for use by either a peer editor or a teacher.
3. A peer conference response form for use by students in response to others' work.
4. A revision response sheet for use by a teacher or a student.

A CHECKLIST FOR EVALUATING COMPOSITIONS
Rating Scale for Quality

	Low	Mid	High		
Higher Order Concerns					
Information	1	2	3	4	5
Significance	1	2	3	4	5
Focus	1	2	3	4	5
Context	1	2	3	4	5
Form	1	2	3	4	5
Voice	1	2	3	4	5
Reader Cues:					
Title	1	2	3	4	5

Lead	1	2	3	4	5

Lower Order Concerns

Spelling	1	2	3	4	5
Sentence Punctuation	1	2	3	4	5
Verbs	1	2	3	4	5
Punctuation/Mechanics	1	2	3	4	5

General Comments:

On Deadline: Yes/No

Grade:

–Created by Dr. Thomas Reigstad

PEER OR TEACHER EDIT SHEET

I. Two aspects of your paper that I liked were:

II. Something I need to know more about is:

III. You need more examples/evidence at:

IV. Mechanical errors in the paper detracted from its clarity in these places:

PEER CONFERENCE CHECKLIST

	Yes	No
1. The paper was read aloud.	___	___
2. Positive comments were made.	___	___
3. Needs for clarification were stated.	___	___
4. Copyediting was done by one group member.	___	___
5. The paper's intended audience was discussed.	___	___
6. The author's voice in the paper was discussed.	___	___

REVISION RESPONSE CHECKLIST

I. Your title was:

II. Your lead was:

III. The construction of your argument was:

IV. Your paper needs more development at these places:

V. You need more examples/evidence for:

VI. Your concluding statements were:

VII. In general, your organization was:

VIII. The paper succeeds in these ways:

_____

APPENDIX D

THE DOMAIN SCORING RUBRIC

The document contained in this appendix is the expanded version of the "Domain Scoring Rubric" which was created in 1986 by the Virginia Department of Education's Language Arts division for use in scoring Virginia's Literacy Passport Test. It is the intellectual property of the State of Virginia. It has been used in this Handbook through the permission granted by Dr. J. Kenneth Bradford, Lead Principal for the Virginia Department of Education. The reader will recognize as the basis for many rubrics for writing, among them the Six Trait Writing System.

DOMAINS AND FEATURES

COMPOSING: Focusing, structuring, and elaborating the writer's message:
        Central Idea
        Elaboration(s)
        Unity
        Apparent Organization
        Organization Facilitates Message

STYLE: Shaping and controlling sentences to achieve purpose of message:
        Selected Vocabulary
        Selected Information
        Suitable Tone
        Real Voice

Sentence Variety

SENTENCE FORMATION: Composition of competent, appropriately mature sentences:
>   Standard Word Order
>   Complete Sentences
>   Expansion through Coordination
>   Avoidance of Run-Ons
>   Embedding through Subordination

USAGE: Word-level features related to standard informal discourse:
>   Inflections (verb, noun, pronoun)
>   Agreement (subject-verb, pronoun-antecedent)
>   Correct Word Meanings

MECHANICS: Symbols and cues that allow understanding of written text:
>   Paragraphing Formats
>   Capitalization
>   Spelling
>   End Punctuation
>   Internal Punctuation

DOMAIN SCORING

In this type of scoring, the observation of writing is divided into several domains (categories), each of which is comprised of various features. Each domain is evaluated holistically, with the domain score indicating the extent to which the features appear to be under the control of the writer. Thus an awareness of the features and their use contributes to the score, but the score is a judgment of the whole domain and not simply a counting of demonstrated features. Some skilled scorers can score for all domains after one complete reading, although scorers may often re-read a portion in order to make a decision about one or more domains.
(This is an excerpt from the original scoring statement.)

Composing
This domain includes focusing, structuring, and elaborating the writer's message. A paper receives a higher score to the extent that is demonstrates the following:
>   *It provides and focuses on some central idea (or feeling).

*It does not stray from dealing with the central idea (unity).

*It has an apparent structure or organization.

*The structure or organization tends to facilitate presentation of the central idea.

*Significant ideas and/or images are elaborated through details and/or examples.

Style

This domain relates to the writer's shaping and controlling sentences to achieve the purpose apparent from the Composing Domain. A paper received a high score to the extent that it demonstrates the following:

*Vocabulary has been selected to support the central idea and purpose of the writing.

*The information selected, manipulated, and presented advances the purpose.

*The tone both fits the purpose and shows an awareness of some audience.   *One can hear some real voice in the writing.

*The writer has used a variety of sentences that interest the audience and suit the nature and purpose of the message.

Sentence Formation

This domain relates to the writer's ability to compose competent, appropriately mature sentences, as observed relatively independent of purpose and style. A paper receives a high score to the extent that it demonstrates the following:

*Use of standard word order patterns.

*Expansion of ideas/images through standard coordinating structures.

*Embedding of ideas/images through standard subordinating and modifying sentences.

*Complete sentences.

*Avoidance of fusions (two or more sentences run together as one without appropriate conjunction and/or punctuation).

Usage

This domain relates to features at the word level that cause language to be effective and acceptable for standard informal discourse. A paper receives a higher score to the extent that it demonstrates the following:

*Inflections (changes in spelling that reflect verb tense and noun/pronoun case/gender) are appropriate for sentence structure and meaning.

*Agreement (subject-verb and pronoun-antecedent) is correct.

  *Words used actually fit the meaning dictated by purpose and sentence structure.

Mechanics

  This domain includes the systems of symbols and cuing devices that allow the audience to easily understand written text. A paper receives a higher score to the extent that it demonstrates the following:

  *A consistent format (indentation or line spacing) allows distinction between paragraphs.

  *Words are correctly spelled.

  *Appropriate end punctuation is used.

  *Internal punctuation is consistent with sentence structure and meaning.

  *Capital letters are correctly used.

APPENDIX E

DIRECTIONS FOR GENERALLY USED WRITING TASKS

The contents of this appendix are sets of directions for generally used writing tasks. They contain specific materials which address the full writing process. They could be reproduced for a class when an instructor decides to use the kind of writing assignment dealt with by each respectively. They are used in this guidebook by permission from Pat D'Urfee of Broome County Community College, Binghamton, NY.

SAMPLE SETS OF DIRECTIONS FOR GENERALLY USED WRITING TASKS

THE BOOK REVIEW

General Guidelines for Writing Book Reviews

A book review, or critique, is a short essay which summarizes, analyzes, and evaluates a book. Most book reviews contain the following parts:

1. Introduction: usually a paragraph in length; includes the author's name and title of the book, the type of work being reviewed, the author's purpose or thesis, and your general attitude about the book. It may also include statements about the author's background and qualifications.

2. Overview Summary: acquaints the reader with the work, not by rewriting it, but by explaining in the major points of the book. Try to give the reader (who presumably has not read it) a sense of what that book is about.

3. Examination: zeroes in one or two features of the book to examine in detail. Brief quotations and specific examples highlight important points and give the reader a sense of the author's voice.

4. Evaluation: assesses the value of the book for yourself, your reader, and your course. In this section of the paper (which is sometimes combined with the Close Examination), you focus on the strengths and weaknesses of the book, as you perceive them. Again, brief quotes and specific examples should be used to support your judgments.

5. Conclusion: wraps things up. The conclusion often includes a recommendation about what type of reader would find the book valuable.

NOTE: Some instructors who assign book reviews have requirements that are different from or more specific than these. Be sure to check with him or her before you begin your paper.

TIPS ON PREPARING A BOOK REVIEW

There are similarities and differences between the published book reviews you see in newspapers and magazines and the ones written by college students to satisfy a course requirement. The professional reviewer usually writes about books which his audience has not yet read. His goal is to analyze and evaluate the book so that other people can decide whether or not they want to read it. As a college student writing a review for class, you are probably working with a book your instructor has recommended. This means that he has not only read the book himself, but has decided that it is relevant to your course material. You might wonder what you can tell him about the book that he doesn't already know; probably nothing. You must realize that he has not assigned this project for him to learn about it. Your task in writing the review, therefore, is to convince the instructor that you have read and understood the book, and recognized its relationship to your course. This may seem to be a difficult task. One way to approach it is to pretend you are writing to your classmates who have not read the book. By summarizing, analyzing, and evaluating the book for them, you can show the instructor that you understand it. This is an effective approach to take, because it allows you, just like the professional reviewer, to address an audience which knows less than you do about your topic.

Reading

As in any writing task, a book review requires some preliminary work before you actually begin putting words on paper. The first thing to do is to read the book–at least twice. (One reading is almost never sufficient to fully understand a serious book.) Read fairly rapidly the first time through; you want to get an overall sense of what the book is about. Don't take notes as you read, although you might wish to make pencil marks in the margin next to passages that interest or puzzle you. (Unless you are using a library copy.)

After your first reading, take a few minutes to jot down your reactions to the book and any questions that occur to you. These questions will help focus your attention as you read the book again. Your second reading should be slower and more thoughtful. This time through make notes of important points. Write down page numbers of passages you feel are important or might wish to quote in your review. (Some students find it valuable to stop after reading each chapter, and to write a short paragraph summarizing its major points. Reading those summaries later can help to identify the recurring themes of the book.)

Thinking "Pre-writing"

Having read the book thoroughly in this manner, you should be ready to start working on your paper. Review the notes you jotted down after your first reading and the ones you took during your second reading. Write down any additional thoughts you have at this time. Now ask yourself, and answer in writing, the following questions, as well as any the instructor has suggested to you:

1. What is the author's main point?
2. How, specifically, has he attempted to prove his point?
3. Is his argument convincing? Why or why not?
4. Is the book organized logically?
5. How does the book relate to material studied in class?
6. Would you recommend it to classmates? Why or why not?

It may seem to you that your are wasting time writing out answers to these questions when you could be writing your paper, but in fact, the more time you spend thinking and writing about the book before you begin the paper itself, the easier it will be to write the review when you actually sit down and begin ... which you are now ready to do.

While all essays begin with an introduction of some sort, the introduction is not the first thing to write. In fact, many writers don't worry about the introduction until they have worked out, in rough form, the body of the essay. When you think about it, this method makes sense because it will be much easier to write the introduction when you have a clear sense of what it is you are introducing. Therefore, it's a good idea to start your writing of the book review with the summary. Then you can work through the rest of the paper, and finally write your introduction. When you do your final draft, of course, the introduction will come first.

In doing a first draft, different writers like to work in different ways. Some prefer to write rapidly, not paying much attention to grammar, spelling, or word choice, and then go back over the essay later, rearranging and correcting what has been written. Others prefer to write more slowly and carefully, working out problems as they go along. Neither of these methods is better than the other. Use whichever one seems to be more effective for you.

After you have written your first draft, take some time off from writing to do something completely different. If you have time, leave the paper alone for a day or two. Even if you are in a hurry, try not to think about the paper for a couple of hours. This allows you to establish some distance from your writing, so that when you go back to it you can respond to it as a reader and editor. Reread the paper slowly and carefully. Does it make sense? Have you given specific examples to support your statements? Will your reader understand what you have written? (Remember to think of the reader as another person in your class who has read the book.) If your rereading reveals any problems, fix them, even if it means major reworking of the project.

The last step is proofreading. Careful proofreading can make a difference of a full grade or more. Proofreading is most effectively done slowly, out loud. Make sure you see what you actually wrote, not what you wanted to write. If you are unsure about your ability to find errors, ask a parent or trusted friend to read through the paper with you.

If you follow all these suggestions, allowing plenty of time for the whole process, you can count on writing a better paper (and getting a better grade) than you would have otherwise. You will also see that many of these suggestions can be applied to other college writing assignments.

WRITING SUMMARIES

What is a summary? A summary is a condensation of material from a text. In preparing a summary, a writer locates the main ideas in the text and paraphrases them; the summary does not provide much detail. A summary is a personal response to a text. Do not include your opinion; while restating the main ideas in your own words, you must maintain the integrity of the material you are working from. To write a clear, accurate summary, you must be proficient both as a reader and as a writer.

Why summarize? The process of summarizing will help you understand what you're reading and remember the most important points. A summary helps your reader understand the material you're presenting–and it also shows the reader you understand.

How long should a summary be? The length of your summary depends upon the length of the original text and your purpose in writing the summary. When you are asked to write summaries for college courses, your professors will provide guidelines for length.

In preparing a summary, you may find the following steps helpful: 1. Reading the text. Scan the text to get a general sense of what it is about. What do you think the author's purpose is? What is the tone? How is the text organized? What are the main ideas? Carefully consider the title, the headings and the sub–headings, the introduction, the conclusion, and any illustrations that accompany the text, such as photos, graphs, charts, etc. Read the article completely, section by section. Underline the important points. Read the article more than once to be sure you understand the material.

2. Taking notes from the text. Your notes should include the purpose of the original writing, the name of the author, the title of the text, and the main ideas. Sometimes you can figure out that the main idea is from the title, introduction, and conclusion; supporting ideas often appear in headings, subheadings, and topic sentences of paragraphs. Even if the organization of the text does not lend itself to that type of analysis, you can still consider the material section by section. Be sure to state the main ideas contained in each section. Write not only what the section is about but also what the section says about what the text is about. You might find it helpful to write one–sentence summaries for all of the section and then a one–sentence summary of the entire text. Sometimes (but not always) you can turn the title into the most general statement. For a persuasive passage, look for the sentence or sentences that seem to sum up the argument: summarize the author's overall claim in a sentence. When you write the summary, you will have to maintain the integrity of the writer's argument, whether you agree with it or not, so it is especially important to note the writer's statement of the problem and the solution. For a descriptive passage, indicate the subject of the description and its key features. For passages based upon research, include the methods used.

3. Reviewing your notes. Check your notes carefully against the   text to verify that you have the most important ideas and that they all relate to and support the main idea.

4. Pre–writing for the summary. The following are strategies for identifying the subject and the message of the entire text or its sections and for organizing your ideas into a summary:

* Ask of the text (in any order) the questions employed by journalists: Who? What? When? Where? How? and Why? Without worrying about grammar, punctuation, spelling etc.,write a response to each question. These questions will help you pull out the essential facts from your reading; they will be most helpful to you when you are dealing with complex material.

* Work from any major statement or idea in the text: look for it throughout the text, and whenever you find related ideas, cluster them around the one you began with. You are collecting related ideas (or ideas that develop from other

ideas) to see where they will lead you. When you go back over your notes, you will then decide which of the ideas are most important, and you will use them in your summary.

* Find the subject and the message. Refer to the cluster and ask, What is the likely subject? What would be its message? By first considering possible subjects and messages as options, you will focus your reading and give yourself a subject to think about and later to write on.

5. Writing a draft of the summary. Identify the text and its author; then present the main idea and the supporting ideas. Be sure to include all the main points. Arrange the ideas in a logical sequence, and express them in full sentences. Insert transitional words as needed to ensure a smooth, easy–to–follow flow. Retain the emphasis accorded to each idea by the author: if he or she devoted equal attention to several ideas, you must also treat them as equally important. You may find it helpful to go back from time to time to the original text to make sure you thoroughly understand the author's meaning. Think again at this stage about tone; it is especially important not to miss irony. NOTE: There is debate among rhetoricians about whether or not a writer should quote directly from the original text when preparing a summary. You may find the text contains a thesis you can quote directly in your summary, if your professor doesn't object. When your are in doubt about whether or not direct quotations are appropriate for your summary, always consult your professor.

6. Revising the summary. Go back to the original text and make whatever changes you need to for accuracy and completeness. Check the organization of your summary and reorder ideas, if you need to, to achieve a clear, logical sequence. Look at sentence structure, and make adjustments as needed.

7. Editing the summary. At this stage, you should look at sentence structure even more carefully. Turn fragments into complete sentences or combine fragments with ideas expressed in other sentences. Do your sentences vary in length? To avoid a series of short, choppy sentences, combine two or more ideas in a single sentence. Get rid of unnecessary words. Check grammar, punctuation, spelling, etc., and correct your errors.

THE MICROTHEME

This MICROTHEME is a writing assignment developed for physics and math classes at Montana State University. It is especially appropriate for science and technology classes, but could be adapted to any discipline. (You saw it earlier in Appendix A in its generic form.) Based on the assumption that if students truly understand a concept, they ought to be able to state it clearly and succinctly in writing, the microtheme requires students to write a concise essay on a 5x8 card, applying a specific concept to a problem posed by the instructor. The responses follow a specific format, helping students to think through and organize their answers, and allowing instructors to read the microthemes quickly to assess student understanding.

Because MICROTHEMES are so short, they can be evaluated fairly quickly. Grades should be based on clarity and logic in dealing with course concepts.

FORMAT

(This is the microtheme format developed at Montana. It could be modified according to the demands of a particular course.)

MICROTHEME

Question: A statement of the problem posed by the instructor.

Response:

Key Idea: A one sentence response to the question.

General Idea: Presentation of the main ideas, terms, and relationships involved.

Specific Case: Application of these ideas to the specific question.

Extra: Any additional insights that further explain the concept.

For additional information about MICROTHEMES, see "A Writing Teacher in the Physics Classroom," by Larry Kirkpatrick and Adele Pittendrigh, in *The Physics Teacher*, March, 1984, pp.159–164.

BIBLIOGRAPHY

Works Cited

Burke, Kenneth. *The Grammar of Motives*. Berkeley: University of California Press. 1969.
-------- *The Rhetoric of Motives*. Berkeley: University of California Press. 1969
Ciardi, John. *A Browser's Dictionary: A Compendium of Curious Expressions & Intriguing Facts*. NY: Harper and Row. 1980.
Cowan, Gregory and Elizabeth. *Writing Brief Edition*. NY: Addison-Wesley, 1980.
Dilliard, Annie. *The Writing Life*. NY: Harper Collins, 1990
Estes, Clarissa Pinkola. *Women Who Run With the Wolves: Myths and Stories of the Wild Woman Archetype*. NY: Ballantine Books, 1997.
Grimaldi, William M.A., S.J. *Studies in the Philosophy of Aristotle's Rhetoric*. Weisbaden: Franz Steiner Verlag, GMBH, 1972.
Harris, Muriel. "The Over Graded Paper: Another Case of More is Less. How To Handle the Paper Load". Urbana, Ill: *NCTE*, 1979.
Kirby, Dan and Tom Liner. *Inside Out: Developmental Strategies For Teaching Writing*. Montclair, NJ: Boynton/Cook Publishers, 1981.
Kirkpatrick, Larry and Adele Pittendrigh. "A Writing Teacher in the Physics Classroom". *The Physics Teacher*. March, pp. 159-164, 1984.
Lindemann, Erika. *A Rhetoric for Writing Teachers*. Oxford, UK: Oxford University Press. 1987.
MacAllister, Joyce. "Responding to Student Writing". *New Directions for Teaching Writing in All Disciplines. Jossey-Bass, 1982*.
Macrorie, Ken. *The I-Search Paper: Revised Edition of Searching Writing*. Portsmouth, NH: Heinemann. 1988.
Neeld, Elizabeth Cowan. *Writing: Brief Edition*. NY: Addison-Wesley. 1986.
Olson, Carol Booth, ed. *Practical Ideas for Teaching Writing as a Process*. Sacramento, CA: California State Department of Education. 1986.

Vygotsky, L.S. *Thought and Language.* Cambridge, MA: M . I . T . P r e s s . 1 9 8 5 .

Virginia Department of Education. *The Domain Scoring Rubric.* Richmond, VA: In-house publication. 1986.

Winterowd, W. Ross. *Contemporary Rhetoric.* UK: Oxford University Press. 1975.

Young, Richard E., Alton Becker, and Kenneth Pike. *Rhetoric: Discovery and Change.* NY: Harcourt, Brace, and World. 1970.

GENERAL

Anson, C.M. "Distant Voices: Teaching Writing in a Culture of Technology." *College English*, 61.3, 261-280. 1999.

Atkins, D.G. "On writing Well: or, Spring the Genie from the Inkpot." *A Journal of Composition Theory.* 20.1, 73-86. 2000.

Bean, J.C., Drenk, D. & Lee, F.D. in C.W. Griffin Ed. "Microtheme Strategies for Developing Cognitive Skills." *Teaching Writing in All Disciplines.* pp. 27-38 San Francisco: Jossey-Bass. 1982.

Boyd, R. "Teaching writing with logic." *College Teaching.* 432. pp 53-56. 1995.

Brostoff, A. "Good Assignments lead to Good Writing." *Social Education*, 43. pp. 184-186. 1979.

Greene, Stuart. " The Questions of Authenticy: Teaching Writing in a First-year College History of Science Class." *Research in the Teaching of English.* 354, 525-569. 2001.

Griffin, C.W. "A Process of Critical Thinking: Using Writing to Teach Many Disciplines." *Improving College and University Teaching.* 31, 121-128. 1983.

Grossman, P.L., Valencia, S.W., Evans, K., Thompson, C., Martin, S. Place, N. "Transitions into Teaching: Learning to Teach Writing in Teacher Education and   beyond." *Journal of Literacy Research.* 324, 631-632. 2000.

Hill, M. "Writing Summaries Promotes Thinking and Learning across the Curriculum-But why are they so difficult to write?" *Journal of Reading*, 34, 536-539. 1991.

Jonsberg, S.D., Dobson, M.H., McCarthy, K., Campbell, M.J., Lovegreen, C.L.N. "What Book or Resource on the Teaching of Writing would you Recommend to Other English Teachers?" *English Journal*, 901, 25-27. 2000.

Kessen, J., & M. A. White. "Writing across the curriculum. Wanted : Guidelines for teaching writing in non-writing courses," and "WAC - an answer to multicultural diversity". Papers presented at the Annual Meeting of the Conference on College Composition and Communication 43rd., Cincinnati, OH, March 19-21, 1992 and the Annual Minority Student Today Conference San Antonio, TX, October 19, 1991.

Keim, Mark C. "Creative Alternatives to the Term Paper". *College Teaching.* 39, 105-107. 1991.

Kurlifoff, P.C. "Reaffirming the writing conference: A tool for writing teachers across the curriculum". *Journal of Teaching Writing*, 10, 45-57. 1991

LeTourneau, M.S. "Text as a linguistic level: Implications for teaching writing." *Composition Chronicle: Newsletter for Writing Teachers*, 97, 5-8, 1996.

Lutzker, M. *Research projects for College Students: What to Write Across the Curriculum.* Westport, CT: Greenwood. 1988.

McMillian, V. & D. Huerta. "Eye on Audience: Adaptive Strategies for Teaching Writing."

Journal of College Science Teaching, 344, 241-245. 1988.

Moss, A., & C. Holder. *Improving Student Writing: A Guidebook for Faculty in All Disciplines*. Dubuque, IA. Kendall-Hunt, 2003.

Nolan, Elaine. "Writing and the Senior seminar: Empowering Students for Entry into the Sscholarly Community." In O;Dowd & E. Nolan Eds. *Learning to write, Writing to Learn*. pp. 19-26. Livonia, MI: Madonna College Humanities Writing Program. 1986.

Roen, D., Pantoja, V., Yena, L., Miller, S.K., Waggoner, E., *Strategies for Teaching First-year Composition*, Illinois: National Council of Teachers of English. 2002.

Sanders, Stephen. "Learning logs: A communication strategy for all s u b j e c t a r e a s." *Educational Leadership*, 42, 7. 1985.

Schiff, Paul. "Responding to writing: Peer critiques, teacher-student conferences, and essay evaluation". In T. Fulwiler & A. Young Eds., *Language Connections: Writing and Reading Across the Curriculum*. pp. 153-166. Urbana, IL: National Council of Teachers of English. 1982.

Storlie, E.F., & M. Barwise. *Asking Good Questions, Getting Good Writing*. Minneapolis, MN: Minneapolis Community College. 1985.

Tchudi, Stephen.N. *Teaching Writing in the Content Areas: College Level*. Washington, DC: National Education Association. 1986.

Zimmet, N. "Engaging the Disaffected: Collaborative Writing across the Curriculum projects". *English Journal,*, 901, 102-106. 2000

INDEX